# Adoptymum

## A SURVIVAL GUIDE TO LIFE WITH ADOPTED KIDS

# ELENA HOLMES

AdoptyBooks
www.elenaholmes.com

AdoptyMum
First published 2019 by AdoptyBooks

ISBN 978-1-910089-90-3

Author: Elena Holmes

Design by George
Illustrations: Elena Holmes

Printed and bound by Scandinavian Books
c/o LaserTryk.co.uk Ltd
Hamilton House, Mabledon Place
Bloomsbury WC1H 9BB

Printed on paper from a sustainable source

A CIP record of this book is available at the British Library.

There are many books for prospective adopters, and this book fits firmly on the shelf for 'must read' books about adoption.

This adoption story adds an approach that is humorous, hopeful and honest.

This is a book of hope, fun and joy, and at times pain and confusion, but always bouncing back to hope.

It is a book about developing Adopty-Resilience – something all adopters, friends and family of adopters and school staff need.

Joy Hasler ·
*Creative therapist,
author and expert on adoption*

AdoptyMum is honest, heartfelt, painful, and funny. I started reading and couldn't put it down.

It is the story of one mum's ( and AdoptyDad's) journey into adoptive parenting, its joys, embarrassments, trials and sheer survival, with an underlying theme of love for and commitment to their children, whatever the pressures.

I would recommend this book to anyone interested in adoption.

Sue Topalian MA
*Creative attachment therapist*

*This book is dedicated to*

My brilliant parents for loving me #teamdadforever

My gorgeous children for inspiring me

My wonderful husband for being the other half of me

And to the legend DH, without whom
we would be childless, floating around the Caribbean,
drinking cocktails and relaxing far more often. Damn it!!

# Contents

To adopted children everywhere

**They may not have my eyes,
they may not have my smile,
but they have all my heart**

Anonymous

# Foreword

By Joy Hasler

There are many books for prospective adopters, and this book fits firmly on the shelf for 'must read' books about adoption. This adoption story adds an approach that is humorous, hopeful and honest. Elena tracks her journey from first thoughts about adoption through five years and looking forward. As an adoptive parent, I recognised many of her descriptions and feelings, but I wish I had had her sense of humour and energy.

The book follows the journey from the pain of learning about infertility – I was also told to 'come to terms with my infertility before adopting a child' – to making the adoption application, through to her experiences with other mothers whose conversations centred on childbirth and baby stages of development. She takes us through school challenges, surviving travelling and holidays to celebrations of progress and developing attachments. Throughout the story, there is clear evidence that Elena has read widely herself, used her training and experience of working with children as a teacher, and opened her heart and mind to new approaches with a discerning streak as to whether these approaches are appropriate for her 'Adopty' family.

Throughout the book are tips and points of interest that come from research as well as from her experience. I would love some of these researchers to read this book to see how their expert advice is put into practice. They might find new ideas and enjoy the expressions of hope Elena conveys. This is a book of hope, fun and joy, and at times pain and confusion, but always bouncing back to hope. It is a book about developing Adopty-Resilience – something all adopters, friends and family of adopters and school staff need. I have known Elena and her family through some of this journey, and thank you Elena for this very readable, enjoyable and personal account of your life as an AdoptyParent.

Joy Hasler MA
September 2019
Music therapist and adoptive parent;
Editor of *Creative Therapies for Complex Trauma: Helping Children and Families in Foster Care, Kinship Care or Adoption*, JKP London, 2017;
Founder of Catchpoint Consultancy CIC,
a registered adoption support agency

# Introduction

A doptyMum is an explosion of thoughts, fears, hopes, sad days, happy days, future days and the worst of all worst days. Over and over and over. And I don't just mean the book, the real-life version is the same!

I want this book to serve as a nitty-gritty guide to being an adoptive parent. During the adoption process you are pointed towards many books to read while you wait. 'Helps the time pass quickly,' they said. It didn't. It terrified us into thinking we can't do this one minute, then yes, we are going to be kick-ass parents the next.

In truth we do both. We swing from being ecstatic parents with brilliant ideas, methods, craft plans, holidays and day trips booked, school bags packed and homework done, to sobbing on the sofa eating yet another bag of chocolate, bereft of any energy other than enough to mumble and scoff.

But I am here to tell you that's OK. And normal!

The books I read really help with adoptive children. Teaching techniques, strategies, giving you templates and guidance. But they don't offer a giant hug and a scruffy-looking person with mum hair, gently rocking and reassuring you that you are amazing and doing a fantastic job with the sound knowledge that yes, they have been there as well. And then some!

We have not been there and done it all by any stretch of the imagination, but I always feel reassured when I meet up with a friend who tells me a worse story, offers me sugary sustenance (I'm not a wine drinker luckily!) and tells me that it will get better.

Because it will. So use this book as a helpful drunk friend

hug. Write in it, highlight the hilarious moments where you thank whoever you think exists that these are not your kids, scoff at it, take tips and hints from a non-judging friendly gal, look at how we've done it and work out what you might do differently.

Laugh with me, cry with me and remember you are amazing. Your partner is amazing. Your kids are amazing, and you are such a strong individual. You are strong enough to handle the cards you have been dealt – so go handle the crap out of it.

Ooh, and if you are an adoptive parent doing it alone – then you are so phenomenally amazing, as I could do nothing without my amazing AdoptyDad. He rocks!

There are moments in this tale where you will disagree with me. But that is right. You should, because I do not have your kids. I have Biggie and Littlie and they are unique. They fit the pattern of millions of children in the world with their behaviours and attitudes, hopes and fears. But they do this in their way, for their reasons, stemming from their own background and traumas. So please – if you recognise your child in any of this book, give my response a go by all means, but remember your child is a crazy individual too, and so they may not work to your plan.

But don't give up on them – they never gave up hoping to find you.

Elena Holmes – AdoptyMum

## Chapter One

# Beginnings

*Our longing for eggs*

*Que será, será*
*Whatever will be, will be*
*The future's not ours to see*
*Que será, será*
*What will be, will be*

T hat was our first dance at our wedding. Picture us, happily performing a lovely Viennese waltz (not quite a Strictly 10, probably a three, at best), imagining all of the good things which lay before us, when my husband stood on my dress and ripped it.

Actually, Himself was exhausted, and I was looking at all the mess I needed to organise cleaning up! But we were very happy. We had everything we needed in our lives including a house, a dog and good jobs.

We both worked long hours, but we laughed a lot. We were happy in each other's company but knew that we wanted a family. We had both always wanted children and the timing seemed right.

We had met six years before. We first bonded over our shared love for the beautiful collie puppy which had been given by a wonderful neighbour to my family. We were also rather nervously overseeing the upcoming nuptials of my best friend to Himself's best friend. They were first in our group of friends to marry, so it was unknown territory to all of us. We both went to the same church, so we frequently bumped into each other at various pre-wedding occasions.

We always laughed and had fun, but as an 18-year-old I didn't see adults as potential husbands, just as much more sensible than me!

After a church weekend away, our love bloomed over a Roald Dahl book. This was despite the fact I absolutely panned him in a reading contest – the entire book took me 8 minutes, him 45 minutes! This is the man with a PhD, yet he can't beat me in a reading contest! After that, the rest was history. Everyone, including our parents, were happy and we started thinking about making a life together.

I conned him into buying a house by accidentally booking a viewing for a sale, not a rental – a genuine mistake, but it worked out well. We bought our first home together in 2006 and moved in ready for Christmas. It was manic, stressful but lots of fun! We were welcomed into the street by a couple who drank seven bottles of wine between them the night we went for dinner. What we didn't know was that they were a pair of notorious swingers but we left innocently unaware of any other plans they may have had! We met the lady next door who bought everything she saw on QVC including a petrol chainsaw which she couldn't even lift and, terrifyingly, was stolen from her shed.

We adopted a dog called Saffron from the same lovely neighbour I mentioned earlier. Slightly awkward conversation: she said she'd left her husband. I replied, 'Can I have your dog?' Luckily, she said yes. We also acquired a giant ginger puppy called Fred. By now I was a newly-qualified teacher, and I brought the school rabbit home most weekends, so we were a happy band of five. But as with most marriages, people like to meddle. Instead of greeting us with 'Hi there, how are you?' the common phrase was 'So when are you going to have children?' When did it become OK to ask people about their sex lives? I would never, ever dream of asking someone something so personal as to when they are going to start having extremely regular and quite mundane sex in the effort to reproduce – so why do others think they can ask me?*

But one day we decided that maybe we were grown up enough. Sure, we still ate ice-cream with chocolate cracking and left Disney movies in floods of tears, but let's just chalk that up as research. We were sensible, not bankrupt, hated late nights and clubbing – it seemed a perfect time to hang up my high heels and hoop earrings and become a mum.**

Unfortunately, we were one of the unlucky couples who just couldn't make babies. We didn't have the agony of losing any, just the frustration of nothing working. We received so many hints and tips on how to get pregnant – get him to drink Ribena, a bottle of wine will do it, just relax and stop worrying about it. Seriously, since when has 'stop thinking about it' ever worked?

We were so disappointed. Would we never have the thrill of seeing the scans of a new life developing inside me? Would I never get cravings for chocolate at 3am and send Himself out for some of the good stuff? Would we never see mini versions of ourselves running around? It seemed such a shame. Mainly because my husband has lovely blue eyes and an incredible academic brain, and I can make outstanding fudge, and these are important traits to pass on to a new generation!

When the doctors start looking into why things don't work, you can't help but blame yourself. I think it must be down to me because I have suffered for years with strange appendix-type pain without an appendix being to blame – it must all be womanly-related. My other half believes it to be him – with no evidence whatsoever to back this up.

These problems definitely hurt. You begin to see your body as a failure. We are genetically made for reproducing, yet my body couldn't do this. I think this is something I haven't ever really forgiven myself for and so even now I hate my body for all of its medical abnormalities – 'typical of me' is the phrase we trot out when something else alarming develops. But we are not the kind of people to wallow, and so we pulled up our socks and got on. We did the doctors, the consultants, the embarrassing tests and the heart-wrenching, exhausting journey which was IVF.

Nothing worked.

I was sat in a hospital bed next to an older woman, waiting like a proud hen to have my eggs collected. My neighbour told her partner, 'They managed to get 20 eggs from me!' Feeling smug, I thought, 'Well, I am much younger so that's great, I'll have lots of viable eggs to choose from!'

No. I got four. I'm sure even my husband could have produced four! And only two were any good. Smugness subsided, and this hen left the henhouse feeling like I might as well be cooked up for Sunday lunch. (Talking of Sunday lunch, if you've never had bread sauce with chicken, go for it. It's a game changer!)

Knowing this was our situation, we chose to look at adoption. Our hearts wanted children and there was no time to lose!

* *For my husband's manly pride – it only becomes mundane after such a long time of trying – never before that, I promise.*
** *Himself says he loves late nights and always hated clubbing – kids didn't change that.*

# Chapter 2

# Humiliations galore

*We learn to swallow our pride
– again and again*

Adoption seems to have become trendy – it's frequently spoken about in the news, on chat shows and it's a plotline in most of the soaps. This is mainly a positive thing, as it helps to normalise our situation. But it can also lead to a lot of misguided understanding from those who've seen an adoptive family in a soap, and so think they know exactly what we are going through. That reminds me of a card I recently purchased for AdoptyNanna on her cancer diagnosis – 'If life gives you lemons, I promise not to tell you about my cousin who died from lemons'. Everyone knows someone who's had something to do with adoption, but sadly it really does not mean they 'get' your life, even with the best of intentions.

Having adopted children is something that should easily be forgotten – the adoption part, not the children themselves, obviously. Becoming a parent in any way is a huge journey, and as an enormous percentage of the world achieves this, it's not something which needs to dictate every conversation and waking thought.

However, when you have adopted children who have had a traumatic start in life, this is just not a luxury you can have – you can never forget the adoption side of your life. You need to eat, sleep and breathe adoption because it is the result of the traumas which your children experienced. Many of the children in the world will not have been conceived through love, though very few remain unloved. But when they are seen as a pain or an inconvenience, emotional connections with that child do not occur. Loving emotions do not flow to the developing child, and this allows insecurity to grow. Low-quality food choices will make physical development weaker than it could be. Stress hormones weave a poisonous path through that new life's brain, creating blocks in the natural pathways, forcing the brain to rewire itself.

All of these are the starting points for the trauma which will forever affect my children. It stimulates their reactions and responses every minute of every day, which is why adoption is never forgotten. If I choose to overlook or not mention how I got the children, it is done when things are going well for them. When things are going horrifically wrong, if I don't remember why it is that they arrived here, then it probably affects my responses to them, and that is when we get cross, not therapeutic.

We have learned to parent both of our children therapeutically. That means we are sometimes very firm with them, but we also allow them to respond naturally to situations and help them develop more helpful reactions which cause them less emotional upheaval. Being cross and asking 'Why did you do that?' is completely pointless as they have no clue why they've behaved the way they have. They have too many emotional explosions occurring in their brains to even begin to think rationally!

The new life we have as AdoptyMum and AdoptyDad is so tangled that some days we barely know what our names are! Life is just so different and it is impossible to picture how it will pan out. You never truly imagine all of the ways that

---

### Therapeutic parenting

Therapeutic parenting draws on an idea called PACE by Dan Seagal. PACE stands for:

**Playfulness**
**Acceptance**
**Curiosity**
**Empathy**

These are the mantras we always try to remember. Using one of these strands when everything is going wrong is a much calmer way of handling issues and allows your child to experience love and acceptance rather than anger and rejection. It's tricky, and you have to work against your instincts, but after the problem has been dealt with, you feel much less angry and hurt by your monsters, in my experience.

Basically, don't react in the same way as your child – after all, what's the point of shouting 'Stop shouting!'

---

your life will change – something as simple as visiting the bathroom alone is one of the weirder things that you will miss.

These AdoptyParents miss shopping at the supermarket. Gone are the days of a trip to the shop without bribery, annoyance, singing, and walking in the way of people. Gone is the freedom to buy whatever you want, regardless of government guidelines on health and Five-a-Day targets. The truth is, on our first night off from parenting, myself and AdoptyDad went to Tesco! We wandered around looking at all the glorious food, trying to decide what we could do with our time off and the saddest thing was – we couldn't think of anything to do, so we went back home and slept. However, it was glorious. Just being us again for a tiny part of the day felt strange, exciting and exhausting. But we struggled to switch off from our new roles. Because our children fill so much of our brains, hearts and lives, we basically exist as walking, talking, calming machines, predicting the next incident that could occur to destroy our day; that rubbish moment which causes the issues that our kids just can not manage.

The worst place for this sort of uptight, on-edge parenting is during play with other children. I'm sitting there quietly simmering, just waiting for something to go wrong.

Because of this I have a tendency to explain everything, just to make it clear why things might go wrong. Desperately trying not to tell strangers too much, trying not to justify my child's behaviour, is impossible. I have found that on very few occasions can I keep the information about how we came to be a family top-secret!

It's normal and healthy for family and some friends to know this information, but strangers? It's tough tough tough to keep it from them; why do I feel the need to explain?

I think it's because of embarrassment. I'm not embarrassed of my children – okay when Biggie sashays around, pretending to be on Strictly, and busts a few of his dance moves in a spectacular Dad-meets-child-meets-daddylonglegs fashion, I may cringe a little. Or when Littlie shouts out to the world in the middle of a church service (topic – Jesus has risen): 'Oh my gosh, why did Jesus go to prison?' I may wish the floor would swallow me up ... but I am never embarrassed for their reactions to situations as they, along with us, are learning to manage them in their own time.

Maybe this is something all AdoptyParents feel? The need to justify myself for my strict parenting is very frequent, but

I know our parenting style benefits my children massively. We've spoken about this to professionals, and they fully support us and our ways. Still, we have people judging, criticising and complaining about the way we do things.

I think I justify myself because I know I wouldn't be this type of parent if I'd been handed a home-grown newbie straight from my nether regions.

Because my children may not react or behave like the average child, I am quick to defend and explain, so the parents don't begin the slow, calm move away with their kids to the other side of the playground.

On one sad day I found out I was being phased out by a group of mums in the playground. It was down to my parenting style. They couldn't see why I acted the way I did, or why my children weren't allowed to behave freely without care. This hurt. I must admit, I sobbed my little AdoptyMum heart out. These parents didn't mean to hurt me but they just didn't have time or energy in their lives to learn more about our situation.

It is so, so hard to break in to playground cliques if you don't join the school at reception stage. The playground can be a tough place for a parent on their own account. We all have our own emotions which are triggered by the sound of a school bell; some adults can't manage those overwhelming feelings, so they keep their heads down.

Others with a more positive outlook on school are happy to sympathise with a smile, but they have generally already found other likeminded folk to form friendship groups and PTA teams. My own mother's playground friendship groups go right back to preschool and antenatal meetings. However, when your kids don't start at the beginning with you, these key social interactions just don't happen. And I don't just mean for the children. Littlie did start school in reception, so she began setting those building blocks into place, but they were already wobbly due to her emotional reactions. And since moving to a different school, these blocks have been completely destroyed. Littlie can make friends because she is charming, funny and happy, but due to her severe anxiety issues, she has heightened emotional responses. She over-reacts in a truly spectacular fashion which, quite understandably, puts most youngsters off!

Biggie didn't used to get invited to birthdays. His behaviour, his noises, his sense of anger and upset got trickled home to the parents by the children. I understand their reasons, and he often drives me to insanity, but I worry for his little heart when I know he's been overlooked for a party invite. It is a rejection which sadly he is all too familiar with.

These rejections are something they will eventually learn to deal with, fingers crossed, because we all face rejection in many forms every day and most of it we can brush off. But think about those infrequent incidents which annoy you, rile you, burn inside and stay with you. This is what rejection is like for our AdoptyKids; it's a massive trigger to revive feelings of their past traumas, so of course their reactions will be bigger. Everyone expects a rescue dog to have trust and behavioural issues, so why wouldn't the child versions have them too?

These issues are comedy gold as well, however. I have experienced so many public humiliations that my life has become like an episode of Benny Hill. They cause me great joy (at a later gin-infused stage of that day) and are shareworthy in a top moments countdown.

**Humiliation #3** At Christmas while we were with family at an animal park, Littlie wiped her muddy wellies on a mat in a Chubby Chase, do-the-twist style, which caught the attention of a visitor behind us. When said visitor repeated the twist action for her own wellies, Littlie exploded. 'Stop copying me, idiot, doesn't your brain work? Why does she have to copy me?' I explained that perhaps the lady had seen her brilliant technique and sought to replicate it with her own muddy boots as it had been so successful for Littlie. The visitor enthusiastically agreed that this was the case. Littlie (unable to take praise when in the midst of an explosion) then shouted, not six inches from the visitor's face: 'Well don't copy me, it wasn't brilliant, it was just obvious!' Then muttered 'You fool' under her breath. I quietly apologised to the lady and tried to move things along. However, the pleasant visitor decided she had to point out the obvious to all of us, just in case we really hadn't noticed: 'Well someone is rude today, aren't they?' At this point I grabbed Littlie with my hand clamped over her mouth and we rushed away as I really wasn't sure who would be first to correct this assumption – AdoptyMum, AdoptyGrandma, AdoptyDad or, worst of all, Littlie.

**Humiliation #2** When in Ikea, explaining the direction to the nearest bulk bag of tealights to another customer, I was loudly admonished by Littlie. 'Mama – stop speaking to strangers, you don't know her, she's a stranger, stranger danger!' I thanked her for reminding me about that rule but explained that it was a way to keep children safe, rather than adults. She did not agree, and when the lady chuckled at the situation – well, it was like triggering a nuclear reaction.

Tiny, innocent-looking Littlie screwed up her face, took a deep breath and began a stream of angry words directly at the shocked stranger: 'Get away stranger, you're not safe, you might steal me, what are you looking at, we are not your friends, it's none of your business, go away danger lady, stop looking at my mum, she's mine not yours!'

In my head I could hear a foghorn on the public address system – 'Extreme embarrassment in aisle 3. We need a huge hole digging in aisle 3 please!'

So I did what any sane person would do. I threw my stuff down and got the hell out of there. I couldn't explain or apologise because technically Littlie was right, plus it's hard to speak through a mix of horror, shame and giggles!

This kind of thing is sadly not restricted to this country.

**Humiliation #1** On a Mediterranean holiday, Littlie found it difficult to adjust. The heat and the unfamiliarity were making her wobbly and of course, the staring public did little to ease her anxieties. Late one evening, in the midst of a screaming fit, Littlie spotted a stranger who was showing some interest in her behaviour. She chose to question the bystander with an extremely loud 'What are you staring at, you filthy rat?'

Our jaws dropped open. How on earth could we come back from that? Thank the Lord that the woman didn't seem to understand the actual words, but I'm pretty sure she got the meaning! Even aliens on Mars would have got the message, especially when it was accompanied with a filthy look, a hand on the hip and a scowl that could kill. Plus the volume – howling wolves baying at the moon have nothing on this kid!

We laugh now, but blimey that was a tricky one to calm down and move on from!

But isn't that the beauty of parenting – they embarrass you now and then you embarrass them? Just you wait Littlie – I'm coming for you!

Chapter 3

# Deciding to adopt

*Trying not to see children
as products on a shelf*

A doption is something everyone thinks they know at least a little about but, as it turns out, nowhere near a tenth of what you need to know!

So we went, one month after our failed attempt at IVF, to an adoption support day run by one of the many agencies that are the professional experts in this field.

It was interesting. We sat and listened, and heard many facts on the number of children in care, how long the average child waits, how hard it is for sibling groups to find a home together, the hoops adoptive parents have to jump through, the assessments needed, the involvement of social services, plus many other mind-boggling things.

We saw several couples leave the event looking encouraged, but many more looked as if they were convinced it wasn't for them. Several appeared to be traumatised, and one poor lady was sobbing. The subject raised such a muddle of emotions – no wonder we all looked terrified.

I decided to be brave and approach the woman running the event. There was a queue, so I helped myself to a few chocolate biscuits for courage – well, it would have been rude not to, they had been paid for (remember this for later!)

Eventually, as I was about to lose my nerve, I got to the head of the queue. Sheepishly, I asked: 'How long after fertility treatment are you allowed to start the adoption process?'

The lady beamed, presumably happy I was asking an easy question, and replied with a cliché: 'How long is a piece of string?' It all depended on the individual and when they felt ready. I sighed, feeling relieved. Test one passed – tick! She then asked me how long it had been for us. 'One month,' I replied. The friendly, smiley social worker turned into a frowning, simmering dragon with steam flowing from her ears.

'One month? You can't possibly be ready. You need to grieve for the fact you will never be a natural mother and accept that you need to take someone else's kids – and goodness knows what they will be like!'

At that point my heart broke, the floodgates opened and my brain exploded.

I muttered thanks and scooted out to the privacy of the car, where I let everything out. I was so hurt that I had opened my heart to this idea and this pain, and the social worker had just stamped on my dream.

I was brokenhearted for a few days – because we were ready. Yes, it had only been a short time since we had discovered that we couldn't have children, but so what? AdoptyMum and AdoptyDad couldn't become parents the regular way, but we were excited to try another way.

In our family, we are Tiggers. We get knocked down and we bounce back up, stronger than ever.

Having had so many medical knock-backs has made me this way. Repeated hospital stays and never getting to the bottom of my problems is annoying, painful and so frustrating. It took more than 10 years before the doctors diagnosed me with endometriosis, yet I'd stayed in the same hospital several times in extreme pain. There was no evidence of appendix issues, yet they always blamed the appendix! I even bounced back when I was given the worst news possible in a casual aside when a doctor dropped in to see me, after emergency surgery, as I sat alone in my hospital bed, with no husband for support and no warning of the blow that was to come. I was surrounded by older ladies who had enjoyed telling me they had just had the same surgery as me.

The doctor checked my notes before tutting and stating: 'Yeah, looks like you won't be able to have kids.' Then rushed off to answer her beeper. I looked up in surprise: 'What? Ummm, was that meant for me? Hello? Me – are you sure …?' My voice tailed off as the doctor rushed away. I am sad to add that she didn't return to explain further. So when I informed my husband later, it was a very unsure, sad prognosis rather than a certain one. Our chance to grieve properly had been taken away through lack of information.

Eventually our sadness turned to anger. How dare the social worker say one month is too short a period to grieve. What does she know? Grief is personal and no one can tell you how long it should last. It's not like there's some huge sadness hour glass, dropping tears until suddenly you get a tap on your shoulder: 'Time's up love, move on!'

When we lost our beloved AdoptyPop (my dad), the grief was unpredictable and continues to this day even after a couple of years. I don't think that one will ever subside.

But the need to have a child that was shared by me and AdoptyDad – there was nothing uncertain about that. So we decided that clearly, that particular agency was not for us. Too many Negative Ninas on that team – we wanted Positive Pamelas!

We began to realise that in the world of prospective adoptive parents, we were a rare commodity – we had the physical space and the willingness to take siblings. In fact, when we attended another adoption info day, we realised to our dismay that it was a parent cattle market. Like lambs to the slaughter we were driven around the room towards agencies waving flyers and photos of children at us. We were intentionally separated so two sets of staff could sell their children to us. I thought it was strange that someone who had just been talking to us shouted from behind and pointed at us. Of course, they were alerting a colleague to our presence as fresh meat, so they could corner us later.

It's easy to understand their behaviour. With government targets to meet in order to keep your jobs, it becomes less about the children and more about keeping the system rolling.

How tragic! Only slightly less tragic than the Argos-style catalogue you can use to choose a child.*

In the end, we chose an agency that didn't have a policy on grieving, and accepted us as we were. Our social worker, Rachel, was the most amazing, patient, wonderful, honest woman. She took the time to learn all about us, really understanding us, seeing our weaknesses, showing us our strengths – even if we couldn't see them ourselves.

At first we were worried because we'd had a visit to check out our home, and were told that our house smelled of dogs. (It's not a smell, it's love.) The home checker assured us that due to the size of our AdoptyDogs – a pair of labradors – we would definitely need a social worker who liked dogs.

Ah. First hurdle, she didn't like dogs. Hmmm, not helpful! Luckily she grew to tolerate ours and even now she asks after them (not often, but she does ask).

Yet we couldn't have asked for a better supporter. Rachel made things happen. True, she never ate the treats I bought for her visits – making me feel like a heifer as I couldn't stop.

---

### Social workers

Social workers who deal with adoption have the hardest jobs. They have to protect the little people in their care while meeting government targets, plus filling in endless paperwork. They have to deal with birth families who may be on the scene, and deciding whether to keep siblings together or split them up. That's without even mentioning all the training they both give and receive.

When they take a child away from their birth parents, they are the worst people in the world.

When they don't act quickly enough to remove a child from a difficult home situation, they are demonised, especially if it ends tragically and the media get involved.

It's key to remember that their job is to help the child first – and that is the most important heart that they need to consider.

---

And the whole process stressed me out so much, I couldn't stop yawning. Each visit was so emotionally draining that we would be fit for nothing when she left.

But she got us there. The things you see at first as picking and fussing, develop into ticks on a checklist. You begin to realise that things in the process cannot go wrong, because Rachel will not allow them to. Thanks to Rachel, we dotted every I and crossed every T. We bought fire blankets, fire extinguishers, built a doggy pee patch in the garden, covered plug sockets, locked down social media accounts, researched schools, doctors and hospitals. We bought thermometers, baby gates, first aid kits, Calpol by the litre and even created a safe haven under the stairs for our pooches to sleep in, away from prodding fingers. All this for unknown children who might not need half of the stuff we had installed.

To prove just how perfect Rachel was for us, she told us that before we had even been approved as adopters, she thought she had found our children. She didn't share much information because she didn't want to get our hopes up, but when we read their profiles – blimey, were they our children. Rachel gave us a video of them and we watched it over and over again, transfixed by our future running around the screen. We were goners. Our hearts had been stretched and two small people had reached up and tucked themselves inside.

*

It is hard to know why we fell for them instantly. I think it would be the same if you gave birth to a child that looked like a potato. You would think they are the most beautiful thing on this planet and that is how we felt. Now admittedly we lucked out. Both of ours are gorgeous kids. Freckles, deep brown eyes, photogenic smiles; one tall, one small with cheekbones to cut glass. But they have happy faces and personalities and this just won us over!

So with these little ones safely in the back of our minds, we moved on to the next step. Going to The Panel.

*The Argos-style catalogue which I mentioned is a regular magazine filled with children who are looking for their future families.*

*They include a mini biography and an image of the child. It is so heartbreaking. There are around 200 in each and it arrives monthly. Over successive issues you see the same little faces in there, which means that they haven't been chosen. You begin to wonder why, and struggle to contain your emotions. You begin to imagine the pain felt by the children who are not wanted, like the puppies in the pound who are never chosen, and begin to hate yourself for not being the one who wants them either. Yet you need to choose the child you can love. You can't force yourself into love.*

Chapter 4

# Attachment

*What do we have in common with puppies?*

When it comes to adoption, the biggest challenge I think you face is attachment. It is a strange, subtle factor which affects every person in the world. It is a fancy term for relationships. It influences every relationship you experience in your life – how it develops, grows, fails, changes and why it does those things.

Take puppies. Noodle, our beautiful pup, was looked after well by her birth mum. She fed her milk and took care of her needs. She did the same with Noodle's siblings. They developed together, learning through play and squabbles, being gently reprimanded and steered by mum when necessary. Noodle was the last pup to leave the litter. This gave her even longer to learn some puppy manners. Mum had more opportunity to deal with Noodle one-to-one, so she clearly knows boundaries and respects them. She had a very secure attachment to her birth mum.

Noodle's litter mates left for new homes up to two weeks before Noodle. So their attachment was probably less secure as they had to share mum's time, affection, teaching and love – potentially moving on before every necessary lesson was taught.

That's an animal-friendly way of explaining the way we all work, humans as well as puppies.

We all have attachment issues, in my opinion. They can be positive or negative. You may be closer to one parent than another. Your siblings may dislike one parent more because they are jealous of your closeness with said parent. You may also be prone to anxieties due to events which happened in your childhood or later in life. In AdoptyWorld, these are known as traumas. And they all play their part in building us.

Our fears are founded on these factors – for example, I am scared of death slides, those vertical slides you get at amusement parks, due to a very traumatic reoccurring dream when I meet my end on a death slide. I can't even look at them without feeling nervous and sick. Maybe you don't like dogs because you were bitten as a child – works in the same way.

So if you have a good attachment, usually based on a secure and loving upbringing with your parents, then you are likely to trust people and see the best in them. You're less likely to suspect people of having ulterior motives, and will be happy to make friends, showing trust to people close to you and being trusted in return.

Imagine a brick wall. You need a good foundation to build a strong wall – with babies the foundations are healthy food, warmth, comfort, interaction, eye contact, love, sound and so forth. When you grow, these needs change and the next level of bricks is required – education, good examples, morals, fitness, plenty of sleep and so on.

If some of the emotional bricks are missing from the earliest stage of the foundations, then the wall higher up will wobble. It may still be standing, but it will be less secure than others that were built more securely, and is much more likely to come tumbling down.

If you do not have a good level of attachment, you will find it hard to put faith in people. You've probably trusted someone in the past, and they let you down. This leads you to become suspicious of other people, and your self-doubt leads you to wonder why they would want to spend time with you.

All this means that you prefer to be in control in most situations so that you can predict every move and do not get overwhelmed by unexpected events. In their birth home, Biggie and Littlie missed out on meals and interactions with safe adults. They were exposed to loud and angry noise, and spent days without anyone speaking to them. During those vital foundation years they had no routine. This makes their brick walls very wobbly. They find even the most mundane situation a threat if their emotions are high.

Queueing, for example, is near impossible. Their anxiety just builds – what will happen when the queue is over, what if the thing they are queueing for runs out, or they won't be able to join in? What if there is a better queue over there and we are in the wrong one? We bounce and fidget, we sing and make beeping noises, we have a tantrum and are rude to people – all sorts of problems can develop in a queue. It's true that many children find queueing hard, but ours are not simply bored. It's because their sense of anticipation is so great that they get excited, but then their negativity (a learned behaviour) creeps in and tells them that it isn't worth the excitement. So they might as well end the queueing situation right now – and the quickest way to do that is cause a problem.

*

Teaching that actions have consequences, and sometimes lead to reprimands, is an extremely tough problem for AdoptyMum. I am much better at it now, but to be a good therapeutic parent, you need to rely on natural consequences. Jeez, that is so hard to get your head around when things are going wrong. A natural consequence is something which happens without intervention – for example, when you refuse to wear a coat, you get cold.

That would be fine if the biggest issue facing me is that Littlie or Biggie refused to wear a coat. But one quick look at my weather-battered, exhausted face would tell you that this is NOT the case!

My natural teaching and parenting style is firm but fair. It was always this way throughout my teaching career and although some children would begin September hating me, by the end of July they were sad to be moving to a new class.

This worked for me. I had many challenging pupils over my years but they had reasons for the way they acted. Gradually we all learned to work with each other rather than against each other. There were some really unusual moments which really tested my brainpower, but my firm-but-fair approach stood up to the job.

Biggie and Littlie present all sorts of tricky situations where it's really hard to hold out for the natural consequences rather than intervening yourself – especially when you know that your own parents would never have stood for such behaviour.

I have heard myself say "You're lucky AdoptyNanna isn't your mum, as I'd have got a smack for that." What on earth? True, but what was I thinking? Not only is it a weird thing to say, and quite threatening, it makes AdoptyNanna seem like a scary ogre. What am I hoping to gain from it?

Never has either AdoptyKid turned around and said: "Good Lord, you are right, mother – we are behaving badly and should have been counting our blessings since the day you walked into our lives, for you simply are marvellous!"

Firstly, if either said that, then I'd have to kung fu their asses as I'd know they'd been caught in a zombie apocalypse which somehow escaped the news headlines that day! (Haha – as if I'd get a chance to watch the news.)

Secondly – why should they say that? They aren't lucky I came to their lives. Yes, they are fortunate to have a fun-loving, sweetie-eating, sometimes-rapping, hard-ass mum who would take anyone down ever if I needed to!*

But they don't need to count nice parents as a blessing. They deserve that. Everyone deserves that. We didn't save them. We aren't special – we just have way more patience than the average loon parent. We just have big hearts and want to fill that heart with gooey squishy adorable wobbly kids. They are the biggest pain in our asses but worth every minute. And every minute we are learning, adjusting and developing our own attachment issues.

I would assume that only a small percentage of adoptive parents develop degenerative brain conditions**. Well, my brain never stops whirring and although occasionally there's also the odd clunk, the constant change brought about by parenting Adopties is certainly a stimulating challenge!

* I can rap one section of one song due to many wasted hours in the common room during my A-levels. However, the joy and amazement on Littlie's face when she first heard me do it will warm my heart forever.

** This could be complete nonsense but a) I don't have any energy to spend on researching it so I shall just hope for the best; and b) AdoptyParents don't make old age due to the large amount of partying they do once the kids move out. (A joke, obviously.)

Chapter 5

# The Panel

*Our judgement day arrives*

If you want to adopt children, you have to seek approval from an adoption panel run by the local authority. The panel is a group of people from different areas of the community. I recall one of ours being a doctor – the rest maybe vicars' wives? I can't remember. Their faces are a blur due to the extreme level of adrenalin that was coursing through my veins at the time. Generally, though, they are mostly people who work in some kind of public service and who have a good understanding of what an adoptive parent needs to look like.

The build-up to this day was so intense. Social services scrutinised every part of our lives over and over. They only put you forward for the panel if and when you are ready. Our house had to be prepared for children, even though we didn't know their ages, genders or even the number of kids to expect. Our families were interviewed to ensure that they were safe to be the relatives of our future children. Even our friends had to give references to our good characters. Thanks to those people by the way – look what you got us into!

On the day of The Panel you dress up smart and travel to the town hall to be signed in and led to meet your fate. Imagine being led past hungry lions dressed as a steak and you might understand some of the tension we felt. We didn't want to arrive too early – so we stayed in the car until we deemed it to be early enough to look keen, yet not too early to look like we were so stressed that we hadn't slept and got ready several hours early and just hung around waiting. Your one friendly ally from social services talks to you briefly, then takes you in to the room and the interrogation begins.

The panel are a group of seven very smiley women of varying ages. They look reassuring and appear to want us to succeed – they are radiating warmth. Then they start to speak. They look at our bank statements and even our receipts, making us kick ourselves for buying several hot drinks at the drive-through last month, surely a complete waste of money to their eyes? They ask questions about child care plans and what support we could call on quickly if things got tough. I practically forget my parents' names at this point, trying desperately to recall who I would leave my children with, and praying I wouldn't say the names of the dogs, even if I think they would make great babysitters.

The panel members are friendly, but formal. It's tough – we are so tense that we stumble over answers, but eventually the questions come to an end. We leave the room and the giant sweat patches we have made on the chairs. Did they like us? Did we answer things properly? Are we financially able to look after a child?

Less than two minutes later we are called back in. Panicked slightly at the speed of the decision, we enter the room on the edge of tears, fearful that something has gone wrong or that things will be delayed.

We are wrong. They are so certain of our ability to be parents that they have agreed unanimously, and instantly. There was no discussion to be had – they knew we could do it. Drum roll please ...

'We are delighted to approve you both as adopters!' The crowds go wild and begin cheering our names ... Actually,

I burst into tears and threw my arms around AdoptyDad while the panel members wiped their own tears away. I don't know why they were so emotional – they knew the answer already! It was a lovely, horrible moment I will never, ever forget. Deep inside that feeling of acceptance remains.

We just couldn't believe it. It was our positive-pregnancy-test moment. Our eight-year journey, throughout which we felt like we could only do things wrong – eight years of failing, waiting, failing, waiting and failing again – was over.

We would be parents. But then comes a bigger challenge – finding a child!

\*

How do you even decide what you want in a child? That's not a normal thing to think.

I was brought up to understand that you get what you are given and be grateful. For most people, that is how it works in the baby-producing world. But not when adopting. You need to think carefully, not about what you want in appearance, but more what you think you can cope with. Can you manage a child with foetal alcohol syndrome? Will a child from a broken home bring up trauma from your own past? What if the child has been sexually abused – can you deal with that?

These were questions that muddled my brain. I hadn't the foggiest what I could manage, and what might create such chaos inside me that I might explode in a giant ball of chocolate and tears. So, I relied on good old AdoptyDad – I could call him that now – who was much clearer on what he thought he could handle. I agreed with his thoughts, and together we looked again at the magazine filled with children waiting for a home. I knew this publication served a purpose, but it was heartbreaking to flick through it and reject children for what seemed like petty reasons. But needs must, to narrow down the search.

Now I know you are thinking 'Hang on, what about the two children your social worker suggested?' But you need to know that it is a competitive world for adoptive parents – several couples may be asking about the same set of children, so we were advised not to let our hearts settle on any particular kids.

Thankfully our moons were in the right aura, or some kind of positive voodoo-type gibberish was occurring, as Rachel, our social worker, rang to say she thought the two siblings were still looking for a home, and could be a match for us. We were given more information, and a longer DVD of them, and that was it. Our hearts were stolen by Biggie, then aged six, and Littlie, just two.

Now we had an idea of who we were about to become a family with, we needed to prepare ourselves and our home. This was the beginning of a lifelong rollercoaster which we can never get off! We took the attitude that the more you know, the better you are prepared. (Actually this is AdoptyDad's attitude; mine is more of 'wing it and see what happens'.) We attended training, we read books, we listened to podcasts, we endlessly discussed how things might go. Even AdoptyRelatives got in on the act by deciding how they wanted to be known – Nanna, Pop, Grandma and so on. We felt as ready as we could be.

We were encouraged to make scrapbooks to sell ourselves and create a narrative for our prospective children to see. Idiots – we'd forgotten to tell the kids that we were their parents! How on earth do you make a life-story for kids you've never met? You do a Blue Peter and thank God that AdoptyMum was a qualified teacher. Felt tips, tissue paper, glitter, stickers, photos and washi tape all came out, and we buried ourselves in Crafts R Us for the next month.

Borrowing from Dr Seuss, we wrote about the places we'd go and the people we'd meet – and, most importantly, the new bedrooms they'd have.

It was now that I discovered the one traditional emotion I shared with a pregnant mamma – nesting syndrome. Because I had minimal ideas about my children's likes and dislikes, I just went with obvious, gender stereotypes with a few unique touches thrown in. So for Littlie I bought puppets, princesses and all things pink. (In fact, she adopted the character of a very well-known blue princess for almost three years and didn't touch majority of the things in her room.) And for Biggie it was Lego, cars and Dr Who. (All of which made him angry, upset and obsessive, leading to him asking us to remove them from his room.)

As I developed my natural talent for nesting, car boot sale after boot sale was visited, searching for the most exciting toys which I wanted to help them play with. Board games I loved growing up. Toys which were expensive new but only 50p secondhand. Cuddly toys of all shapes and sizes, including a Care Bear each – siblings for my beloved childhood friend who sat on my bed waiting for a game. The most exciting part was the zoo we built, a cage filled with cuddly animals of all species, ready for the kids and I to learn about while we bonded.*

We finished the scrapbooks with photographs of their new bedrooms, their new family and some outdoor toys which we had been donated. We couldn't wait, and the days sped by until that first day in September when we would meet the new members of our family with the foster parents. I won't go in to the introduction process as it was a painful experience, which is unlikely to be the same for any of you. I was battling severe allergic reactions to our newly painted home and struggled with meeting my future family when I had a face like Shrek**. There were awkward power struggles between us and the foster family, who seemed keen for the children to move out, while at the same time being reluctant to hand them to us. Let's just say if I didn't see the foster parents again in my life, then I would be OK with that.

It amazed me at the speed in which Mama and Papa Bear mentality kicks in, even during these first few visits. You move from seeing the children get told off, and feeling worried that they are difficult, to thinking, 'Get away from my child, you nasty witch!' It took just hours for us. I vividly remember having to rein in Mama Bear when I heard my son (eek) get told off on our first visit to a soft play centre, and watched him missing out for rest of the session – around 30 minutes. I hated every second of his little sad face filling with tears. So I made the effort to get to know my son (eek)

---

### The family likeness

I am a massive believer in nurture rather than nature. Frequently we are told how similar Littlie is to me in looks. Biggie is a mini-AdoptyDad in personality and interests. The eye sees what it wants to see, and unless your children are vastly different in ethnicity, no one will know the difference!

who promptly began chatting nonsense to me. He hasn't stopped yet!

Our time allotted with the children increased each day. We experienced bedtimes, meals, outings and then sleepovers. Each one of these was terrifying, because you have to start as you mean to go on – firm but fair, remember – but you also don't want them to hate you. (We shouldn't have worried. Biggie now hates everyone*** and Littlie loves everyone, so we've not done too badly!)

During our introduction period – only two weeks long – Biggie was charm itself. He didn't refuse anything, didn't cause more than a whiff of a problem and was a great chunk of giggly happiness to be around. Littlie was a ballet dancer who leaned in a ballet pose everywhere we went, danced her first dance with Daddy (to be repeated at her wedding, so she said), destroyed all board games with a smile and had to be dragged from the dogs' beds on several occasions.

So far, so good. We – and the children – had leaped every hurdle. The kids were bewitching. We were bonding – a family in the making.

*It was never played with, and we sold it all while I sobbed.
** Sadly not an exaggeration.
*** Put it down to pre-teen moodiness.

## Chapter 6

# Friends

*Not the one where they'll be there for you*

What a minefield. Friends are the best thing in the world, and the very worst thing as well, sometimes. Everyone has had a good friend in their life. My childhood friend is the love of my life and I can't wait to enjoy another 30 years at least drinking cocktails with her.

If you think of friends in circles, you have close friends who don't need to know there's a problem, they are close enough to see it or feel it. Then there's the next ring of friends with whom you share laughs, sadness, meals and general chit chat, catching up as though no time has passed.

On this same circle are the people you can rely upon to pick up the kids from school, grab something from the shop for you or come to the movies.

Then there's the social media circle, who were friends in some form once, and now you are not so close, but you still share your life events with them. So they sit in the followers section and enjoy the weight losses, the holidays, the cute new pets and anything else you show off to the world and his wife.

Everyone else isn't on a circle. They float around, sometimes paddling towards your inner circle, sometimes drifting away.

But for some weird, backward, hurtful, unfair reason, those in the closest circle are the ones who hurt you the most.

Newsflash: I am too sensitive. I find the world a painful place. The news upsets me. Happiness makes me cry. Animal love breaks my heart. Facebook makes me sob. Pride floors me. Arguments send me to my bed in floods of tears. Wearing your heart on your sleeve is tough. The minute I feel left out of something, or I feel like someone doesn't like me, AdoptyDad has to practically scrape me off the floor, stop my tears and remind me that I am a good person. And sadly this continues to happen.

Friendships are tricky. Which is why, when that close group hurt you by excluding you, not communicating but not telling you why, pushing you out, ghosting you and judging you – it hurts so damn much.

All your fears and worries flare up and you find yourself doubting your very purpose. Because after all, if the people who know the very bones of your family and the tough times you have, can't stay friends with you, it must be your fault in some way.

Experiencing this made me realise the kind of pain my kids suffer. They push those closest to them away to avoid that same pain I'm feeling.

They have needed that skill for their very survival on this planet, and they exploit it regularly as a shield to protect

---

### Drill for friendship emergencies

**Step 1** Walk away from the upset.
**Step 2** Eat some chocolate.
**Step 3** Remember, it's not you, it's them, and you are brilliant.

---

their already broken hearts. So on those days, when I sit feeling sorry for myself that yet again I've been a doormat to someone I considered a good friend, and maybe also ponder why Biggie and Littlie can't make or keep friends, I need to remember that skill. Maybe it should be given at birth to us all like a parachute.

We give this advice our kids so often. Don't worry, they probably didn't mean it. Never mind, there's lots of other

### Top tips for friendships

• Don't buy friendships with material items. It never lasts.

• Don't offer to decorate someone's house with them. We've lost four sets of friends this way and genuinely are baffled how it went wrong – we are really not that bad at decorating!

• Do offer lots of laughter opportunities - everyone feels better with a smile.

• Eat with them. Eating breaks down barriers as no one looks hot when they chomp!

• Be there when you can, but look after yourself too. You're no use to anyone if you're broken down!

• Remember sometimes it is them, not you, and that's sad for them as you are fabulous.

• Try to find at least a couple friends of a similar height. All of mine are at least 6 inches shorter than me and we do look stupid if we walk side by side!

• Remember the best times and don't dwell on the bad. They won't all happen again.

people you can play with. But we never take this advice ourselves.

Gradually, through love, we are gluing over the breaks in those innocent hearts. Bits fall off and get knocked and chipped and even new cracks appear. But love, consistency and repetition is the glue that these kids need to help them build their closest circles. Only then can they begin to think about those on the other rings and how to be happy without getting hurt by them.

Chapter 7

# Moving in

*We get to know each other*

Our kids came home (aww, home!) just two weeks after meeting us. That seems an insanely short time to get to know someone – clearly social services' motto is In At The Deep End. We had to land on our feet, and hit the ground running. So we started with a crowd pleaser – a trip to McDonald's. On the way home from the foster home, we pulled in to buy Happy Meals, and took one of the saddest and sweetest photos ever. A photo of our two children, with terror in their eyes but happy expressions on their faces. They were putting on such a show for our benefit, and it breaks my heart to look at this picture as they must have been so scared. Biggie, because it was yet another set of carers for him – he had been living with different foster families for four years – how long would it be before they moved him on from here? Littlie, because everyone she had known in her life was now behind her, probably never to be seen again.

I couldn't have done it. To leave my parents, my toys and my routine would have been too tough for me and now when I imagine the situation, the floodgates open! However, they managed this beautifully. We sat awkwardly smiling at each other, making play with the Happy Meal toys. Soon we were ready to make the final transition – into their forever home.

My heart beats just remembering this. The children raced into the house, Biggie upstairs to his room and Littlie straight to the dog's bed. It remains the same to this day – Biggie comes home from school and goes to his room – to check his things are still there –while Littlie greets the dogs and takes them into the garden, showing them love and that she has not forgotten them. It is funny how I've just noticed this when it's been a constant occurence!

We left the kids to make a mess and show each other the exciting new toys they had. We dealt with minor conflicts when Littlie would take a toy from Biggie, making him upset. We reassured Littlie when she hurt herself three times in the first hour, while mentally high-fiving each other that our social worker wasn't there to point out the non-child safe areas that our new toddler had discovered! (She fell over a toy, bumped her head on a book and fell backwards during an angry tug of war with Biggie.) But they both seemed happy and we sat down sighing with exhaustion, ready for our first night as parents and protectors of two small beings.

We were left facing the tricky problem of when to introduce the children to other people. Years ago, adopters were encouraged to hide away for at least a month after a

### The greatest actors

To look at my children you wouldn't see any of the negatives I've described. They put on a great show, with charm, cuteness and real interest. When we explain that things are tough, you look at us as though we are mad.

Yet Biggie and Littlie are black-belt ninjas in the art of hiding their true feelings and fears. This is true of most adoptive children. They hide the truth so that you don't think badly of them, and perhaps reject them. They've learnt that from a young age, cuteness wins over intelligence. Maybe the cutest got the nicer food? Maybe Cutie stayed with the birth family longer, rather than being put into care.

Adoptive children also know the best ways to not be forgotten, avoiding the risk of neglect. Talking, asking questions, making noises, noticing haircuts and giving

child arrived, to allow them to become fully enfolded in your attention and love. But now, when social media allows everyone to know everyone's business most of the time, it is harder to keep the inquisitive folk from knocking at the door, and ringing up, sending emails and texting over and over again. So, we decided to gently bring people in.

AdoptyNanna and AdoptyPop came by. They brought gifts and witnessed the high-energy performance that was Biggie. He showed them toy after toy, and after being asked to allow them to rest a minute, threw an almighty fit and took himself off to the thinking step – several times. It didn't work. Of course, he needed to show them his toys, how else do compliments are excellent ways to make yourself stand out without making people too angry.

Because others don't see the negatives, it is hard for people to believe they exist, help you with them, or care about the difficulties. You begin to worry that you are the one causing the issues. At times I felt like I had gone mad – why couldn't AdoptyDad see the issues Biggie and I were having? Getting one parent on your side is another tool in their armoury. It keeps them safe.

Unluckily for mothers who are the main care-givers, the kids tend to hate Mum. Not you, just the 'mum' figure. We aren't the biological house they lived, grew and felt safe in, and we never can be. It's a battle you can't win. So, for your sake, I suggest you don't try. Adopted children don't mean to hold on to this perfect person, their ideal of a birth mother; their heart does it automatically.

you make friends? Now we look back and realise we could have handled it differently. We were so worried about being consistent that we thought we had to be firm-but-fair all the time. However, we work much harder to be therapeutic parents now, and choose our battles wisely.

Littlie took part in the first grandparent home video with AdoptyPop, as he tried to fix her new book after she ripped it apart. This was when we discovered her love of Sellotape. The girl is obsessed with it and uses it on a daily basis as a staple ingredient in her crafting diet. We love to look at this video as you can see her stubborn side from the very start, as well as her love for her new AdoptyPop beginning to blossom.

Even now she remembers him in her own special way – by lifting her t-shirt and saying, 'Ooh put it away, you'll scare the horses!' Clearly something he had said to her a few times.

We met AdoptyAuntie and Uncle in the park. We thought it might go better outdoors as there would be space for the kids to run and play and ignore any new family being forced upon them if they wanted. This was a success, and I would highly recommend this method of introductions. It avoids invading the kids' new territory, and allows noise to be made and adrenalin to be burned off. We had a nice time in the park. We had some challenges from both: Biggie chose Uncle over Daddy several times, demonstrating his issues with attachment. Meanwhile Littlie chose to run as fast as her little legs could, right across the park.

This attachment issue is tough. We were told that we had to give Biggie and Littlie every drink and piece of food, to teach the children that Mummy and Daddy were the ones who would provide for them, and they could rely on us. This was because their birth parents were often not around to feed them, so they took food from wherever and whoever they could. We had to try to prove to them that this set of parents were their one-stop shop for all the essentials of life – especially food. But this is incredibly hard to instil in others, especially when the children are so charming, you can't help but give in.

We faced lots of challenges to our authority over the first few weeks. Gradually these died down, although it took a very long time for Biggie. This is to be expected after being in care for four years – it is so hard to change the habits of a lifetime. It is like someone asking you to not chuck your keys down on the new table, after you have thrown them on the old table for 20 years. It doesn't come easily, and you will often forget. Skills which prove to be useful and keep us alive are ones that we will repeat. Sadly, Biggie learned early on that asking for food doesn't work if there are never adults around to provide it, so he had to find food for himself.

One day we found out just how well Biggie was managing this impulse. Parties with buffet food were a nightmare, as he would sneak back to the food table again and again to gorge himself with unfeasible amounts of provisions. If he was asked to stop, he would get angry and there would often be an explosion. Finally, at a recent party, we thought he was getting to grips with this particular temptation, and we praised him. We told him how proud we were and that it must be tricky to understand the feelings in his tummy aren't hunger, but nerves. We wondered aloud about how well he had conquered his feelings by not taking so much. He promptly replied, 'Oh, I just get the two plates you let me eat and then ask other kids to bring me some more food when you are not looking!' Then he ran off to play.

Flabbergasted, we looked at each other, with no clue how to respond. Stealth mode 100, survival skills 100. He won that round!

Chapter 8

# Protect and survive

*Looking after our loved ones is a complicated business*

The ability to become a mama bear is inbuilt inside every woman. It rears itself the moment her child is threatened. Growling, chasing, batting problems away – she appears ready to fight to save her offspring.

It worked for me – despite having never grown any children, I've got these two's backs, and woe betide anyone who crosses me!

I don't chase predators across forests, baring my teeth and chasing them up a tree. But I have been know to tell off teenagers for bad language in front of my young (Littlie then tells me off for being impolite). I will stop dead in the road and refuse to move if a car is expecting me to mount a pavement to let them pass – I wouldn't accept someone running over my children in this way, so I will not do it myself.

And I am well known for standing up for my kids at school when their needs are just not being met. Because they need me to, and I'm their mama bear.

However, I've recently wondered if some of this protectiveness is necessary, or just coddling my own anxiety.

Recently I saw a pool lifeguard pick up a child who was very tearful. I instantly thought – where is her mum? It's more than his job's worth to touch a child, especially one in a bathing suit. But he did, he comforted her and sent her on her way – and the mother thanked him for his kindness.

This happened in Spain, where people are more open about physical displays of affection to strangers. It made me feel guilty for thinking it would be wrong for the lifeguard to cuddle her – a common  assumption in the UK now, when any physical contact could be deemed as inappropriate and potentially worthy of a criminal investigation. But in other countries, affection and touch are seen as a natural kindness, shown to everyone you meet.

This is certainly something my children could use a lot more of. We were told to try to make sure that they only received physical affection from the two of us, rather than the wider family, as AdoptyKids need to learn that their new parents are the ones to love and take care of them. In reality, this is extremely hard to manage. In the early days, we had to stop both of them hugging absolutely anyone or being overfamiliar. These days our biggest problem is trying to stop Littlie kissing every dog she meets. I am often found shouting across a park 'Don't kiss that dog!' The owners usually tell me that it's OK, their dog is friendly, and I quickly reply, 'Don't worry, I was more concerned for your dog than my child!'

Another way we find ourselves protecting our kids when other families do not need to is at the cinema. There is a really useful website, adoptionlcsw.com, where they have a regular blog, Adoption at the Movies. It reviews kids films from a trauma-based point of view and alerts you to movies which may cause triggers.

For example, take Finding Dory, the lovely Disney undersea adventure. To a regular family, it is a great sequel to Finding Nemo, in which Dory gets her own happy-ever-after. But if you look at it with a trauma brain, you have a character with learning issues (very common in adopted children, due to poor development or parental input), who is without her

## My child doesn't need your biscuit

Did I miss the newspaper story? It seems to have been announced somewhere, without our knowledge, that our kids are public property!

Seriously! People act in the craziest ways. I think they hear the word adoption and think, poor angels, I must spoil, cuddle and save them from their terrible lives. People have told our children they can do things even when we've told them they can't. They've given them food when we've tried to explain that it's important that all the food comes from us. After church one day, an elderly lady witnessed Biggie having hysterics when he was refused a second biscuit before lunch. What did she do? She brought him a biscuit, and then proceed to cuddle him as though we were the bad guys! Would she do this to anyone else's child? No! Insane!

We did not adopt these children as a collective – on their adoption certificates (and on the household bills sadly) are our names only. So why should we share this parenting role? We realise that with birth children, everyone, especially grandmothers, feels free to give their opinions and advice. You can take it or leave it, knowing they do have some idea about bringing up children themselves. However. No-one, including their birth parents, has ever properly parented these children, because they are not regular lovelies. These are children who have suffered severe traumas in their short time on this planet and so have strong and unpredictable reactions. We have been taught how to handle these events and so we really are the best people to do it. We live with them. We see them day in, day out, so we can tell - mostly - what has caused these explosions and how best to return things to normal.

Yes, often we appear at a loss. That is while we recall our training, maintain our patience and calm our brewing emotions - we are human, after all. We have buttons and they are being pushed tag-team style, so we have to respond, in any way we know how, to control everyone's emotions at once.

From now on, when you hear adopted, try to think, 'Ooh, I bet he's a tricky pickle now and again, how can I support those loving parents? Or - 'They've rescued them and are returning those children's experiences to a more normal family life - how can I help the parents feel appreciated for that tough job?'

We love it when people offer to help us, by meeting for coffee, drinks, meals, hugs, calming words, rants, smiles, tissues - and especially chocolate - but we do not love it when we are judged for not doing things your way, or when our children are parented for us. It shifts the power balance to one which unnerves the kids and can trigger even bigger reactions. You may know how to cope with a regular child who's secure enough to feel loved when they are exploding, but we don't have any of those in this house!

So, the best suggestion I can give is to feel free to drop round for a cuppa with a packet of custard creams and enjoy being part of the adult tag team. The kids are not the ones who need you, because they've got us!

birth family (the same loss as for adopted children), where she is the cause of being alone due to her forgetful brain (adopted children are not the cause of their being taken away but they certainly blame themselves and feel the same guilt and shame as Dory does). Dory then goes through life growing up without her birth family, relying on others for help until finally she is accepted for the way she is (a worry that lurks inside many adopted children). Eventually Dory is reunited with her birth family (not always a happy moment if it occurs in real life) and then they all live together happily (never that likely in the real world).

So, looking at that film you can see many opportunities for our children to feel guilt, shame, worry, upset, and feelings of abandonment, jealousy, sadness and large amounts of pain. Which is why my children haven't watched it – I decided that they were in too vulnerable a state at the time it was released. Similar emotions can be triggered by The Lion King, where Mufasa dies and Simba gets the blame. In 101 Dalmatians, the puppies are taken from their birth mum. Dumbo is removed from his birth mother. The Star Wars prequel Solo shows a young Han Solo and his vagrant friends forced to steal to survive. In Show Dogs, one of the dogs is inappropriately touched and, to my amazement, he is told to 'zone out' and ignore the unwanted attention – the very reverse of the advice we give children today. Even Peter Rabbit shows Peter's birth parents dying, and Peter is rejected by his human adoptive mother when he is 'naughty'.

Of course, these potential triggers for our children exist everywhere in the world, not just in movies. It's impossible to work out how much we should try to protect our kids and how often we should simply we face these issues together, to expose them to more of life's challenges. Thankfully the website mentioned above offers you the chance to look at potential triggers and even gives you a few ideas for ways to talk these issues through.

Don't be under any illusion: adopted children's reactions to these triggers can be severe. It might not be merely tears, it can be tantrums, violence, sobbing, self-harm, revenge, sabotage and regression of emotional age. Simply, the triggers can be so damaging that they may not be worth evoking.

Something that most adopted parents will recognise is being accused of being overprotective. Every time I'm trying to caution one of my children about something, I get someone telling me 'not to worry'. It's true that making noise, aggressive play, silliness, snatching, mean words, greed and excessive exuberance are all perfectly normal in children of any age. But because we have to be on guard against the potential for horrendous overreactions, we often find ourselves shamed for our protectiveness, either intentionally or unintentionally.

In a swimming pool recently, AdoptyDad reminded Biggie of the 'No jumping' rule. Biggie stopped jumping in and things were fine – for a while. Around five minutes later he jumped in again. Again Dad reminded him that he shouldn't be doing it and asked him to share some reasons why that rule is there, to help him understand. A further 10 minutes down the line, Biggie jumped in again, splashing everyone and dragging his sister under the water. AdoptyDad then got cross and asked Biggie to sit out for a minute to calm down. Another mother called over, saying 'Don't worry, kids should be allowed to have fun, it's fine.' Thus undermining AdoptyDad, and giving Biggie a huge smirk and told-you-so expression on his face.

The problem is, it's not fine. In our children, things can escalate quickly. One minute Biggie is jumping in the pool with a big splash but causing no harm. Then it's jumping with a rubber ring, then jumping in on top of people with a bigger rubber ring. The next thing you know he is screaming and shouting, running as fast as he can to do a massive cannonball right on top of people and creating a situation where everyone is put at risk including himself. And all within five minutes! Because Biggie and Littlie cannot regulate their emotions, the excitement of a certain action becomes less of a thrill and so they need to take things to the next level.

Another place where this overprotectiveness occurs is with food. We were advised from the start to be cautious with Biggie and food. With his birth family, he never knew when he would get fed. Hence he tends to gorge, stuck in the mindset that he might not get another meal for ages. The social workers' advice was that he should only take food from us. He should always come to us if he was hungry or thirsty, thus helping him learn that Mummy and Daddy will always provide for him and he doesn't need to seek food from anyone else. However, we've been shot down so many times when we try to remind him of this publicly. If we see him eating someone else's food, we remind him that he needs to ask for food. This has been a frustrating lesson to instil in him and it took many years. Kindhearted people would say 'Oh it's fine', 'Let the growing boy eat' and 'You are such a fussy mum!'

Then there was the ultimate heart breaker – one unknown couple reported us to social services for withholding food from Biggie, supposedly starving him. We don't know who they are or what they heard about us, or thought they saw. But their complaint, quite understandably, triggered an investigation by social workers – even though we were following their advice. The social workers knew us, and understood our situation, so the investigation was brief, but this was an extremely painful and shame-filled time for us. People we thought might support us were going behind our backs rather than speaking to us. I felt like an evil monster who was so off-putting that any adult with a concern about our children couldn't approach me. I felt extremely low and really struggled with my confidence in the playground and with developing 'mum' relationships – something I am still very much without.

Those people who reported us, whoever they were, and anyone else who judged us to be strict or even cruel parents, were not meaning to be unkind. They were simply looking at the world through their own eyes. They have no idea about how, for our children, minor incidents can escalate to major traumas. Now it is probably a stretch to imagine Biggie stealing food with a weapon because his friends won't share lunch with him, but it happens, and kids with survival instincts as strong as his need a lot of support and repetition to break them of that instinct and help them develop new strategies for coping.

So I have learned to live with being seen as an overprotective parent. Stuff it if you don't like the way we parent. And knickers to you if you don't want to be my friend – I am a published author and all-round lovely person and I will soon be top of the bestseller list for non-fiction (readers, thanks for your help with this but if you can spread the news of this book further, I would be even more grateful!)

Chapter 9

# Under the weather

*We learn not to be ill*

In sickness and in health. These classic lines are lovingly said at weddings across the world every day. Including at AdoptyMum and AdoptyDad's special day. Although I believe this was the moment I gave an audible sob – did I sense this would be a prominent topic in our lives?

Nope – it was pure coincidence. Another strange coincidence of that day was that our dog, who had attended the nuptials and been silent the entire day, chose her moment to intervene. When the minister said 'What God has put together, let no man, woman or animal put asunder!' she barked so loudly that everyone assumed it was a recording we had played for a joke!

But health hasn't been a strong point of mine. I wouldn't say I was a sickly person – aches, pains and migraines seem to be my bag rather than coughs and colds, but if I get ill, I tend to do it in spectacular fashion.

'Go big or go home' seems to be apt. Twice now a cough I've endured has turned into pleurisy – an illness so Dickensian that you don't expect to encounter it in the 21st century. Luckily my doctor was from Africa and when she suspected a blood clot on my lung, she was happy to inject warfarin herself, being used to doing this as the only doctor for several hundred miles.

My appendix was unceremoniously ripped out when exploratory keyhole surgery revealed endometriosis. This was the first of several bouts of surgery and it took such a monumental twist – I was expecting keyhole cuts, not a giant wound to my abdomen ruining my plans for bikini modelling (I jest, there was no such career!)

A stomach pain on my right hand side turned out to be a huge cancerous-looking tumour on the left which, when removed, took with it a fair portion of my internal organs. The doctor casually said "We will check cancer markers as it is so big." I nodded and blanked this moment out but luckily on this occasion I had taken AdoptyDad with me. Upon hearing this bombshell, he asked – 'Sorry, checking for what?' I had no clue the Big C was even a possibility. Thank goodness it was just a large cyst, rather than anything more sinister.

I banged my head – and it turned into a minor bleed on the brain. My mother always said I'd be silly when I grew up and on this occasion I agree. I didn't even see a doctor or mention the head bang for four days until I began slurring my words, midway through a staff meeting at work. Luckily it wasn't too bad, I must have a hard head.

My much-admired fluid retention was in fact an extra kidney and an overactive bladder. I have never been a bathroom visitor. Some people – who shall remain nameless – pop to the toilet as soon as they arrive anywhere. But I never needed to and the fact I have a duplex kidney and a hard-working bladder seems to make sense! Just more typical AdoptyMum behaviour.

That's without mentioning the other duplicate bodyparts that had somehow developed alongside my regular reproductive system! I am assured I was not a twin who I decided to munch in the womb but I can see why you might think that!

Unfortunately, even with all these conditions, I don't have

time to dwell on my own health. In fact, when writing this I really had to think hard to recall all the details. Illness with Adoptykids is a whole new ball game. You can't afford to be unwell because of the anxiety it causes your little ones. They feel vulnerable and exposed when you are weak, because it could remind them of a time they had to look after their birth parents in a similar lying-on-the-sofa way. They may believe they won't be fed, as Birth Parent may have been too poorly to feed them regularly. It might even trigger them to steal food.

If you're ill, their routine goes out the window, the one thing they cling to in times of stress, because they know where they are with life when it follows a pattern.

If you are ill, to AdoptyKids it means your needs will be put above theirs for a short while, which reminds them of more past trauma, when their parents' needs came first all too often. Illness means less focus will be on them, and people who are not noticed, get forgotten. That's what life may have taught them, anyway. You may be so unwell that life changes for the whole family and they simply can not manage change. Worst of all, you might be too unwell to look after them any more so you will have to send them back to foster care.

Can you imagine living with all of these worries in your brain when your mum or dad gets a simple cold? No wonder they act up. Their brains are so wound up by all of these negative ideas that there is no room for care, compassion, happiness or love – which then upsets the poorly person more!

The one time I genuinely was very poorly, Littlie still managed to grab the attention. I had caught a stomach virus and been physically unwell several times. I had that yucky

## Toilets

Toilets fill me with dread: toilet etiquette, noises, conversations and dreaded toddler talk! But now it is worse as Littlie frequently tells me to stay outside so I don't see her 'privaties'. When I hurriedly point out I I want to stay outside, she rolls her eyes at me and tuts while I turn red!

As we became parents only a short while ago (and ours were biologically produced elsewhere!) my kids have not seen me in the buff. That would be random and very weird to me. As a self-conscious worrier I would rather die than let strangers see me undressed, and in this sense alone, I count my kids as strangers.

When you have a conventional start to your family (tummy babies) the kids grow up alongside you, enjoying access to your delicates when necessary and with limited embarrassment. However, as I am not a tummy mummy, no child has had access to any under-swimsuit bits and so I am in the desperately embarrassing situation of Littlie learning more. Thank the Lord she can now be trusted to visit bathrooms alone, even if you do have to go in and rescue her from the hand lotion massage and blow dry she is giving herself!

hungover feeling in my tummy and was lying on the sofa feeling rubbish and enjoying a small amount of fuss.

Littlie felt sad for me and told me she would look after me. She climbed on to the sofa, wiggled her way up my back and gave me a huge hug. She snuggled into my neck and

WHOOSH – she vomited all over my head, my back, the floor and the sofa! Talk about taking my attention. We then had to clean her, clean everything and stop her tears flowing. Typical.

Oh, and did I mention, she had just eaten a bowl of fruit! Recycled fruit smell doesn't not fade quickly, despite the quantity of shampoo used. Neither does the tale, which she likes to recall publicly with regularity!

Of the two children, illness marks one of them as a survivor and one a flaker. Littlie is like a limpet who clings and cries and is often sent to hospital to double check that it is nothing serious. Biggie is a survivor. He refuses to be ill and won't accept any comfort or kindness, preferring to get angry with me instead because he simply hates feeling vulnerable. He has, however, had two spectacular illness moments. First, he broke a bone in his foot at school and so was put in to a plaster cast. He was eight. We were worried that he would get frustrated but he was very pleased and excited to have crutches. Wrong – we were right first time. After two days he had terrorised the teachers at school, frightened them by running on a damaged ankle, sliding down the banisters, and trying to rip the cast off. So I did what any sane parent would do – I called the hospital and got the cast taken off after four days. It was just such a stressful time for everyone and as the break was very minor, we decided it would be better for him to limp for life, rather than put up with one more second of the frustration. (Not really, he was never going to have a limp.)

The second occasion he was poorly, he completely freaked me out. He cut his finger with a pair of scissors and came to me to get some help. I did the typical mum thing and told him to suck his finger while I found a plaster, which he did. What

I didn't realise is that he seems to have a phobia of blood. He turned a very pale shade of grey and as he muttered 'Mummy I don't feel …' he passed out on the floor before having a mini fit. I was stunned and unsure what to do. Thankfully he came round in 30 seconds and we spent the rest of the afternoon curled up together as he sobbed with fright. It was a really vulnerable moment for him.

Luckily there were no lasting effects, except we do not let him near blood or the taste of it without a giant cushion underneath him! But I've never felt more out of my depth as an AdoptyMum than that moment.

This is a feeling that poor old AdoptyDad is beginning to understand much more since his own health issues started to flare. At a glorious family wedding where he knelt to take a photo, he somehow damaged his knee, causing major issues for at least six months. He couldn't walk faster than a toddler, let alone play with our children. This made him feel incredibly down and worried for our future as a family. He was frightened he might have to take a backseat.

Thankfully due to our wonderful NHS and some mighty strong medication, AdoptyDad has become relatively fit and well again, and although he has flare ups, and he needs to keep away from germs as much as he can, he is back to cycling to work and generally playing the giant papa bear role he enjoys.

Chapter 10

# School days, Part I

*We try to educate the teachers*

For most, school days are some of the best days of your life. You stretch your brain, filling it with new and sometimes interesting information. You're tested by the insanity which is Pythagorus's theory, with the insistence that it'll be useful (almost 7,000 days later, I've still not used it.) And you meet people who may be with you forever – I met my favourite person, Emily, aged six, and we are still great friends now, almost 30 years later.

Being in school teaches you to manage yourself, your behaviour and your belongings. For many, it's the first time that you are away from your parents, which of course is an extremely tough thing to do. Unless you're AdoptyAuntie of course (my sister), who on her first day of school didn't even notice that our mum had left her, and only cried when she collected her because she then realised they had been apart all day!

All of this may not be the case for AdoptyKids though! Fear, anxiety and terror can lurk in the unknown, capable of creating a tidal wave of emotion. There's the playground politics, the problem of making friends and, more tricky, keeping friends. And for each AdoptyChild there is the big conundrum – do you tell your classmates that you are adopted? I feel like I am lying if I don't tell people that the children are adopted, but really it's their story to tell, not mine. Both of mine tend not to tell people, although Littlie occasionally tells others: 'I am a bit different because my mum took drugs'. Of course she doesn't specify which mother this might be, or that it is not the woman they see on the bench in the playground, but if people tell me that Littlie has shared this information with them, I hastily add more context.

My children's school years are the worst days of my life, and we've had them for five years so far. When they came to us we found a school for them, not far away and seemingly understanding of their needs and the potential problems which could occur. We were pleased and confident.

#howwrongcouldwebe

The first blow came when we learned that the headteacher who had shown interest in the children's problems with attachment, and used the right words when questioning us about our kids, had decided to move on. Selfish, self-centred swear word. With bated breath we waited to see how school would go.

**Week 1** I was informed Biggie was the most polite refuser they'd ever had. When asked to go to assembly he told them 'No, assembly is not really for me, but thanks for asking.' They didn't know what to say to this! So every day they had a polite and rather weird standoff with Biggie about anything and everything.

**Week 2** I was reported to school for 'dragging' Littlie to school. Now this is simply not accurate – have you ever tried dragging a toddler? Tantrum-enraged screaming and hitting was happening the whole walk to school so I put her down and held her hand. Apparently this is dragging and had to be mentioned to the school – even though she wasn't a pupil.

**Week 3** I had to fireman's-lift Biggie from the building because they couldn't cope, and he wouldn't walk.

Thankfully the weeks didn't continue like this but at the

beginning, they were mostly awful. Tears, stealing food, running, screaming, barricades, threats, room destruction – Biggie pulled out all the stops.

School staff came out to speak to me every day, and what's worse, they did it in front of the other kids and parents. The shame levels were humungous. Biggie ran off, embarrassed, and I stood there dying, looking at the parents watching and listening in, a purple beetroot glow developing as I was told what hard work my child was and how much he was ruining everyone else's learning.

I felt humiliated and so, so angry. How dare this kid behave this way. As an ex-teacher, I always knew I would find this part of parenting hard; my behaviour expectations were high and I felt ashamed that my own child couldn't manage at least some of them.

Schools are oblivious to your stress, however. They weren't bothered that every time they spoke to me, I physically shrank as they approached, as though I was the naughty child. I felt ashamed of myself because I couldn't bring this child up properly to behave and show respect.

This is completely cobblers (to use one of my father's favourite expressions). Biggie's behaviour and lack of respect was no reflection on me as a parent. He was trying to tell those teachers that he was scared and overly anxious but just couldn't work out how; he didn't have the words to do so. But for some reason these people just could not get that. They knew better and were determined to throw every trick they knew at him until both they and him were exhausted and hating the situation.

The problem is that trainee teachers are not taught about problems with attachment. Attachment issues exist in everyone, whether positive or negative, so the basic

**Top tips for schools**

• Suggest that the school office give a heads-up on any new parents so people can make an effort to introduce themselves;
• Never tell a parent how bad their kid has been in front of anyone else. It just reaffirms to the child that they are bad, and to the parents that they are not doing a good job;
**Final top tip** (this one is to school staff)
• Do not leave the keys to the school within sight of AdoptyChild. He will take them. And lock you out of the room. And laugh about it. Also do not ring me expecting me to help – that's ridiculous. Houdini I ain't!

information could be used to support so many children in school. But because teachers haven't been taught about it, they don't really believe it exists.

We moved Biggie to a highly recommended school six miles away from home. Many adopted families attended there (and since we starting recommending it, many more now do.) He pulled out all of the stops again, but they just asked why? Every time his behaviour changed they would be curious and ask him about his feelings rather than deal with the behaviour. They were firm and fair, with consequences when necessary, but always supportive. They helped us as a family, through regular meetings, bringing in additional support through play therapy and a learning mentor. Best of all, there were no phone calls. They didn't need to call me really to explain any difficulties, they dealt with them and moved on. Unlike his previous school, this one didn't asked him not to attend a trip or insist that I came as well. They even took him to a theme park without our help. They were wonderful from start to when he finished, and now that Littlie has moved there as well, we know they will get the best out of her.

Biggie has now moved on to secondary school, which of course presents its own challenges. I went there recently to do a presentation on Biggie to try to get the facts across. I'm pretty sure if a child told you "I am afraid of the dark!" you'd remember it. If their mum told you "My child is afraid of the dark", you probably would believe it and remember it. However, if you read in a book that most kids are afraid of the dark, you might not take it so seriously. We pay more attention to individuals and their problems – when we know what they are. So I tried to explain a bit more about Biggie to the staff, to make them realise the difficulties he encounters every day.

Maybe some of it went in, maybe most didn't. But a few people looked affected and like they were interested, so maybe that's the best I can hope for.

I wait for a phone call from school on a regular basis. Last time Biggie's school rang I went in to panic mode, thinking they were about to tell me something bad. That means I just never relax. Even if there's no incident to report, the fear is in there waiting to catch me off guard and drag me down. School sucks.

And another thing – why are parents so mean? No one will let me in their group. I've been a mum for five years now and I have zero mum friends from the current school. I get that when you start a school midway through a year then you are an outsider. But come on. I'm an outsider because:

- I can't share birth stories;
- I don't know what antenatal is;
- What the hell is a doula?
- I didn't get a baby like yours that was cute and cuddly but had terrible colic so that we can sympathise with each other;
- I've no clue about growth charts;
- I'm keeping secrets from everyone about the kids' history.

Don't make me be an outsider because I am new to the school too. Invite me to join the PTA – notice my little lost face and smile at me. Honestly – you may be the only person to do so that day!

---

**Don't do this …**

*Both true stories from my teaching career*

• **Teachers** If a pupil brings a carrier bag of kittens to school to give away, please see the funny side, and praise their kindness for trying to help the animals. Then enjoy a large glass of wine that night – they don't teach you about these circumstances at university, and there is no right answer.

• **Parents** Do not offer your kids' teacher Class A drugs at a parents' evening. It's not the ideal icebreaker you thought it was, and it makes for awkwardness every time you see them.

Chapter 11

# Forms

*Life in triplicate*

The 21st century has given us robots digging on Mars, self-driving cars, a little box called Alexa who answers your every whim and the ability to use your mobile phone as a bank card. Yet AdoptyMum's world is dominated by forms. I fill in, on average, eleventy two every week.

Forms for school, on which I realise I have written the same date for the last week and a half, because it's the only one I could remember.

Forms for restaurants – online boxes to complete to book a table before the devil himself appears you asking you to tick the boxes with road signs on. (This week it asked me to identify all of the images with cross walks on them – what the hell is a cross walk? I took a guess that they meant zebra crossings but after four failed attempts I gave up and rang them instead.)

Forms for all types of purchases – eBay, Amazon, Asda, Facebook – even Apple TV requires me to type the 27-digit password my husband deems 'safe', just to watch something new.

But when we realised we couldn't have children, we were completely blindsided by our free lifetime membership to the *Keep handy a black Biro, write in capitals at all times, and be careful not to sign your life away,* paperwork club.

It makes sense. I appreciate every bit of help which results from the paperwork – and I know the senders hate these forms too. But Jeez, let up would you! Altering my favourite quote slightly, I feel like running around saying 'There's a shortage of trees in this world and guess which one's gonna get it?' Since we began the journey of adoption we have completed so many forms. Infertility details. Parenting details. What type of child you think you can handle details. Answers to tough probing questions. Participation in adoptive courses forms. Applications to adopt. Then applications to adopt the specific loons we have.

Then you apply to change surnames for everyone, sign them up to the doctor, dentist, optician, school and nursery. Then you apply for certificates to prove you are a legitimate family. And so many more!

Then, because our kids are typical AdoptyKids with all manner of issues, we have DLA (Disability Living Allowance) forms to complete every couple of years. We fill in assessment forms for all sorts of therapeutic treatments, plus school versions of these.

I don't want to think about the percentage of my life I spend filling in forms of some kind. Repeatedly. It's like they exist for a minimal amount of time, then vanish, so they have to be done again. Maybe they live in that special unreachable place along with the other sock and the Tupperware lid?

Due to my medical issues, I return to the hospital about twice a year and I can't help but feel irritated when they ask if I've had surgery. This even happens when I'm about to meet the kind cutter whom I last met when I was in the altogether in a hospital gown and sexy NHS stockings. It's like those forms have never been completed, and they've no idea what has occurred in my 35 years. So I sit there struggling to recall the details of my eight previous surgical events and when each happened. AdoptyNanna has been having her own issues with forms lately too. She needed chemo treatment and was asked, many times, to complete a Next of Kin form. As I was often with her, I would quietly tell them to add 'widow' to her marital status before a keen doctor or nurse notes she lives alone and thinks it's a powerful female statement of independence, rather than a devastating necessity. But the most recent Next of Kin form was just bizarre. The lovely staff always read them back to you. So AdoptyNanna heard "Next of kin" – followed by the name of my deceased father with the completely spurious statement that he had emigrated. AdoptyNanna, quick witted as ever, responded "You'll have a hard job getting hold of him where he's gone!" She had a chuckle about it but blimey – what a mistake!

If it's not written forms that need filling in, you're being asked for information verbally, and in great quantities. I've probably made it clear that I cannot hold information back easily, yet I am still regularly surprised by the amount of questions you are required to answer, time after time.

When we fly, we always ask for airport assistance due to the potential for long queues. This is something we cannot do at all. It triggers such anxiety in Biggie that he begins hopping all over the place, poking and prodding. We start to fear he will announce he is carrying a bomb, just because he wants to know what will happen if he says that! Littlie will become so anxious that she begins to misbehave, running off, having a strop and hitting her brother, all for something to do. Our anxiety levels start to rise as we become conscious of the tutting adults around us. Worse than tutting adults, however, is staring children. Kids are inquisitive, and the chance to watch a show performed by another child is too great a temptation. And so one by one they begin to watch. Kids also have a resting scowl face. (They aren't being mean, their thoughts are just betrayed by their faces.) But as I am sure you can predict, Littlie doesn't like this. So many times now she has shouted at staring children: "What you looking at? Stop staring at me!" quickly followed by an insult about the child's hair or clothing. Did I mention this would be at full volume with real malice in her voice?

However, much of this is remedied when you ask for special assistance from the airport staff. They rush us through security and baggage check-in to a quiet area where we can be ourselves – as much as my patience will allow of course.

But to get this we have to explain why we need this help. Several times. In varying depths. Over the phone to the Support department. Then again to Baggage. And again to the supportive person leading us around the airport. Then again at the bus to take us to the plane.

Of course we understand the need for these questions and explanations but they dominate our lives and infuriate us. We need giant signs that follow us and point, labelled Unusual People Coming Through. That would certainly be quicker and as I've mentioned, I'm frequently embarrassed anyway!

However, this additional help can occasionally backfire. Just for your amusement, I'll share an example.

When we boarded the Disneyland bus, taking us away from the hell on earth that we had endured (see chapter 15) Littlie was very impatient and began kicking the back of the driver's cab. I used all my skills to try to get her stop – playfulness, firmness, tolerance, understanding, distraction. Finally I held her feet still.

Nothing worked. Littlie was fed up and keen to get home where everything was safe and ordered. Of course, the poor driver lost his temper and shouted at her in French. Thank goodness she couldn't understand him otherwise she would have shouted back! However, the Support lady quickly intervened and explained to the driver that we weren't normal – using the French word "retard".

Oh joy! I died a little inside. How brilliant. My child has just been described as retarded – and by the way, fellow passengers, we are all on your flight home! Big thumbs up and cheesy smile!

On that occasion I didn't explain anything and we kept our heads down, praying she would sleep. And thank the Lord – she did.

---

**Top tip for extra help**

Many kids who are adopted will be entitled to Disability Living Allowance because, as the rules say, "The child needs more support than a regular child of their age."

It might be a small amount, but it really is a form worth filling in. The extra money could pay for a cleaner to save you that precious time needed for a moment of self care.

Disability status helps you jump queues at theme parks and airports, avoiding the dreaded waiting which can invoke a reaction which could destroy the happiness of everyone within a 50 mile radius.

And it could be the very form you fill in which alerts you to just how much your AdoptyLoon needs some extra help.

---

## Chapter 12

# A year with Littlie

*A tough little warrior*

Now you will have noticed that a large percentage of my stories involve the ball of chaos that is Littlie. Could it be that I love her more? Or that we spend more time together? Or that Biggie is so boring I do not have a funny story to tell?

Of course not. None of the above – Littlie came to live with us when she was pre-school, much younger than her brother, and so I spent the next one and a half years with her every day, so we got to know each other pretty well.

Firstly, she is all sorts of crazy. She says the weirdest things and often alternates her accents between TV American and those of my colleagues – Alright Babes and Scottish. She is a wonderful mimic and I often think she's like a young Peter Kay. She has sass, comic timing, compassion and a lot of love for those around her.

If we eat out, she has been known to save leftovers and ask the waiters to box them up for her, so she can give them to anyone homeless. She has questioned me very publicly about why the homeless lady on the floor can't come and stay in her room with us as she does have a bunk bed and she wouldn't mind sharing. She has even sobbed hysterically when she tripped over, dropping said leftovers, which meant the homeless couldn't have them.

Her heart is too big for this world; it's definitely at risk of being hurt – big style. But, as her AdoptyDaddy says, 'I feel sorry for her first heartbreaker,' because they will feel the wrath. The poem 'When she was good, she was very very good, but when she was bad, she was horrid' could have been written with her in mind. Little Miss Feisty Pants is here, she is here to stay, and she is going to take a few of you down along the way.

Our time spent together at home was generally ups, with a daily down. But this was normal as she didn't know me from Adam – or Eve, I suppose, as the mum figure. I told her I was her Mummy and she seemed happy enough about that, but she had to learn about motherly love, having been in care almost all her life.

So that was my aim. To bring Littlie up to school age with experiences, knowledge, fun and lots of love. We grew to love certain TV shows together, singing along happily. We watched classic Disney movies – though I was always anxious about any triggers they might cause, such as the loss of a parent in The Lion King. But I needn't have worried – in fact when poor Mufasa fell to his untimely death, Littlie looked me straight in the eye, shrugged and nonchalantly said: 'He's dead then!'

When we watched The Little Mermaid – an all-time favourite – Littlie remarked that Ariel's mother wasn't anywhere to be seen. I hesitated, worrying that this might remind her of her own birth mother. Again, I needn't have been concerned – apparently Ariel's mummy had probably just popped to the shops for snacks.

It shows that I did too much worrying for her. Yes, she fell over every single day at least 10 times, could barely reach the toilet

> **Top tips for embarrassing moments**
>
> • Laugh loudly and continue your day. Or laugh loudly
> and explain any issues as a good parent would. Or
> laugh loudly and awkwardly, then get the hell out
> quickly. The others around are not judging you, or your
> lady bits they've just overheard being discussed. They
> are holding in a laugh and thanking all that is holy that
> it isn't their beloved child with the questions.
> • Explain the concept of breast feeding before they see
> someone doing it. The look of horror and disgust on
> Littlie's face when she finally grasped where the baby's
> lunch was coming from was also a tough one to ignore.
> It definitely caused some murmurings! She knows it's
> the norm, but it wasn't something which happened to
> her, so she is bound to be a little surprised.

and regularly fell asleep in her food, but she was a tough little bird, and would physically manage any challenge.

On trips out, things got a little trickier. Taking her out of her new safe space – our home – could cause tidal waves in her brain function. Oh, the tantrums, the tears, the screaming – and sometimes Littlie got upset as well. (Ha ha!)

She seemed to be on a time delay, and it was often when we returned home that she would throw herself face down, crying like a child who's lost their toy, begging to go home.

In fact in one video I made of her behaviour (you all know you've filmed a tantrum too!) you hear my bewildered little voice saying 'We are home, look – this is our sofa and our dogs, you are home!' with no idea what to do. Returning home seemed to trigger all of the emotions she had been holding in all day and now that she felt safe, bang! There was an explosion inside her, unleashing the fury within. Many times, she let rip her anger in public, as you can read in Chapter 2 – feel free to enjoy some laughs at my expense. But more often the comedienne within was released, with quips coming left, right and centre. This often took me aback – I wanted to laugh but it wasn't always appropriate, and there were smirks all round.

Here are a few of her classics for you to enjoy and sigh with relief that you weren't involved. (Bear in mind that these were all said at full toddler volume, and when ignored the volume increases!)

• On her first journey on a bus, she ran screaming to the driver shouting 'Stop, there's no seatbelt, we are all going to die!'

• She told off the man at the museum because the bones didn't look bony enough.

• 'Ooh Mummy, what colour pants have you got on? Let me see – ooh, black. Does Daddy like them?' (Not even sure why she thinks that matters!)

• 'When Auntie Chloe had her baby, she pushed it out of her bits – have you got bits like that or do yours not push babies?'

• 'Mummy, are you weeing, because I can't hear you and we don't want to stop on our journey' (cheek of it!)

• 'Mummy, that lady did a huge fluff – ladies don't do that!'

And my most painful and embarrassing of all (apologies for any imagery conveyed):

• 'Ooh Mummy, what's that? It must be a beard. Do all ladies have beards? Will I have a beard? I wonder if that lady over there has a beard on her bits? Shall I ask that lady about the beard on her bits?'

Eventually the dreaded school days approached but I felt better knowing we had done so many things together during our special Mummy and Littlie time and that she had been prepared for the big bad world of school by being filled with masses of love.

Chapter 13

# Sunday, Monday, happy days

*We appreciate the good times*

We have many, many happy days in our AdoptyLives. But as the greatest philosopher of modern times (Ronan Keating) once said: 'Life is a rollercoaster and you just gotta ride it'.

Life in the AdoptyHousehold is exactly like this. We are up and down more often than a whore's drawers – a classic Grandma line. If things are going well, we know that the plummet part of the rollercoaster is coming. This is mainly due to self-sabotage from the kids, and this is something that many kids with trauma do. They just can not bear to feel good about themselves or enjoy what they are doing as it feels so alien to them. When their thoughts are always negative and angry, it feels so strange to them to be happy that they quickly ruin things by acting up, so that the balance of their lives can resume and they can feel at ease once more.

It sounds so mad – why would they thrive in chaos and negativity? Because that is how they have survived – they have lived for many months or years like this, and come through the other side. So they have become comfortable and expert at living this way, and feel happiest inside when things are as they expect.

This is a feeling that gently mends. They begin to stop sabotaging and start allowing us to have these lovely happy moments – but they are few and far between.

Seesawing is another thing we do. When one child is

being 'good', the other is struggling. This is common, I am told, but it definitely makes life tricky.

We can generally get the struggling one onside by being playful. The 'good' one joins in and laughs and of course that is irresistible to a moody child, and so they gradually start coming over from the dark side to the light.

It does, though, make you feel as though all isn't right even when it is going swimmingly! Recently we had a happy day. One which should have been the mother of all awful days – due to tantrums, anger, anxiety, nerves, fear, tension, stress, tiredness, competing for attention, attachment problems, clingyness and just general AdoptyBehaviour – turned out great!

We woke (I slept in!) and the two kids entertained themselves, playing in Biggie's bedroom. He wasn't exploding. He shared without complaining. She played nicely without fuss. They were quiet without being asked. They didn't moan. I felt a little scared.

As you can probably can grasp, life isn't usually like that for us, especially not on a day like this, which was the end of the school holidays. The dread which comes upon each and every one of our household at this time means that we are all a bag of nerves. Last year I found myself giving in to every whim purely to prevent any rocking of the boat.

But not this year, and I was not sure why. Biggie was about to head off to school while Littlie had one more day with me before she had a home visit from her new teacher. We went to the park in the morning for a lovely play (except for the accident Littlie endured within seconds), then we came home for lunch – delicious homemade mummy soup, which Biggie insists I could sell and make a fortune – and then we settled in for a rainy movie afternoon. Biggie then created a plan (my suggestion) for dealing with potential problems at school. He thought about how to deal with them and how his brain would be feeling at that point. He did a fantastic job, coming up with tips and pointers for himself, and he decided that he would check it the next day if he felt a tricky moment brewing. I do not mean to be ungrateful for this day of peace, but from past experience it would usually be the calm before the storm. Let's just keep our fingers crossed for a storm on a British scale rather than a tropical monsoon, tsunami or hurricane!

On these occasions I am merely surprised by the serenity. Is our PACE model of parenting beginning to have an effect? (Playful, Acceptance, Curiosity, Empathy.) Are the games we have learned and practised through Theraplay beginning to soften our terrified, grumpy children up a bit? Or is the creative therapy, which Biggie enjoys, starting to allow him to feel safe and comforted in our home?

Whatever it is ... Thank the Lord above, Hallelujah, Praise Be and all other sorts of classic celebrations including the almighty traditional – WOOHOO!

Other times our happy days are more predictable, organised and full of expected pleasure rather than any surprises. When things happen out of the blue it tends to create worry in the children as their traumatised brain begins to remind them of other times that things happened unexpectedly – and some of those memories won't be positive in the slightest.

So we tend to work with happy moments instead of happy days. There are millions of these and far easier to recall.

• The time Biggie made a toast 'To Love!' and Littlie made her own toast: 'I love this!" while holding up some sweetcorn.

• The time Littlie was enjoying cuddling the boy dog

until she spotted his 'privaties' and questioned 'What's that?' – answering herself, 'It's a bum!" before I had a chance to respond.

- When Biggie went off to camp and got on well.

- When all four of us went away for the weekend and swam together in a river rapid.

- The many movie nights we have shared with pizza, sweets and a great choice of family film.

- The fact my children love Indiana Jones and will ask to watch The Last of the Crusades rather than Temple of Doom – recognising quality at a young age.

- When Littlie ran and gave Biggie a huge hug on seeing him return from Beaver camp.

- Littlie's brilliant overnight stay at AdoptyNanna's in her mummy's old bedroom.

Plus so many more. These seem like insignificant or obvious happy moments but it is just never that easy in our lives. If we feel too happy we get scared, so we change the mood around to bring back the chaos they feel more comfortable in.

## Pets

Pets are the souls of a family. They are with us through good and bad, and despite costing a fortune in vet's bills and masses of anxiety when they become unwell, they are the most wonderful addition to a family home.

We have quite a number of pets, both guinea pigs and dogs. Our older labrador has helped raise our children over the last five years, with nudges, kisses, tear licking, cuddles, warmth and plenty of games. Then the newest addition – a puppy of the same breed – brought much giggling and fun to our lives. The children have seen her grow and have begun to meet their responsibilities by helping us to provide for her – food, comfort, even cleaning up the garden.

It's known that pets can be very therapeutic for children with difficulties of many kinds, because they are giving creatures who don't hate your cross words, and don't worry about your appearance, smell and stresses, and both of our children use our pets in different ways.

Littlie uses them as a friend. She trains them to do tricks in the garden, she talks to them, admires them, comforts them and enjoys their love.

On the way home from her first day at school, she paused, raised her face to the sky and shouted to our first, by-then deceased dog: 'Sabrina, I had a really good day at school. I did drawing and played so much!' It set me off in floods of tears.

We've even got a video clip of Littlie as a

preschooler singing 'Row, row, row your boat' holding the dog's paws while rowing back and forth.

She says that when she grows up she will own many dogs, along with cats, horses, rabbits and unicorns. In fact, I can recall as a child discussing with my best friend how we would have houses with a room for each type of creature.

Biggie uses the animals differently. He doesn't play with them or seek them out but he does find himself sat on by one or other dog quite often. He can't sit on the beanbag without being climbed all over before one or both sit down on him, or very close.

The guinea pig is small and so is allowed more peace and quiet from the children. We've had several and as they don't live that long, as each one has passed away, hysterical sobs have ensued followed by a funeral service and a proper burial with homemade headstones. Having them has taught the children how to handle delicate things, and that small animals can bite! Now we have seen a third guinea pig pass away, the kids are now strong when it comes to pet bereavement so they are more likely to be able to scrape me up off the floor when our beloved dogs go.

However, this wasn't always the case. We surprised Littlie with some guinea pigs on her fifth birthday and she exclaimed 'Pets? For my own children to have? Awww thank you!' Now I'm not sure on the life expectancy of the average guinea pig but I'm pretty sure it's not more than 20 years, so we explained they were for her. She was disappointed that her children would never meet them, but cheered everyone up by reading the pigs a bedtime story every night for at least a week.

Our children enjoy our pets; we can see a calmness come over them when they are with them. Their loyalty works both ways and there is enormous mutual love between them all.

So as long as you supervise your pets and children together then I would recommend AdoptyPets to all. They encourage so much love in to the home and give so much more. They will love you unconditionally and make your family whole.

## Chapter 14

# School days, Part II

*I learn not to be needed*

I'll put my hand up and admit it. I was terrified. What am I going to do without her there with me? Who will I talk to or eat my lunch with? I don't know what to do first or where to go.

I had, as my mother pointed out, first child at school nerves. Biggie started midway through a school year, much older than reception year, and had got the school routine relatively sorted in his own mixed-up, reluctant manner. But it really felt as though it was too soon for Littlie to be leaving me for her first day.

I was devastated, even more so because I felt that I'd let the year slip by without making the most of every second of her time. Yes, it's true she is a weeny nutcase. But she's my weeny nutcase who I understand instantly. She refers to an event or comment in the way a close friend would – 'You know, the thingy' and I get her meaning straight away. My nutcase, whose sentences I explain to others, who are unlucky enough to not understand her the first time.

Up until then I had been the major influence in her life and I was sad that it wouldn't be that way any more. I'm not her friend, and never have been, but the thought of her asking others for opinions and discussing her future wedding, Disney princesses, parental careers, Wallykazam being ugly or even why 'privaties' are called 'privaties', breaks my heart.

I don't know if it's harder for AdoptyMums, because

we've had less time getting to know them than tummy mums, but I know that day, when she left for me for the first time, I was a wreck.

Please do not feel the need to tell me that this was too extreme and that she would be fine at school. It wasn't her I was worrying about – it was my heart that was breaking!

Littlie was over the moon at starting school, and I felt excited to see her make that grownup step towards independence, but I felt frightened at the prospect of not being needed by her in the same way. Is this normal? We seem, as a society, to frown at the attention seeking people who appear on reality TV shows, but maybe we are all attention seeking, or attention needing as social services call it.

How does it feel not to be needed? I should imagine it feels pretty lonely. I can't begin to think of the damage it could cause to one's self esteem. I am sure that we are all needed by someone every single day. Even if it is as insignificant as holding the door open for someone, feeding a pet, answering a question in the street. We are all needed.

And that is why adopted children find their early life so traumatising, I guess. When I see birth parents with their babies they are speaking to them, walking with them and laughing with them in high-pitched voices, making silly faces and using strange made-up words.

But what if you haven't had any of those things? If the person at home no longer notices you exist? Or is too busy prioritising their own needs? It causes anxiety, nervousness and sadness. Neural pathways which develop through sound or interaction, just won't when there is no interaction occurring. You won't learn to trust others because during these vital early years, when your brain is a sponge, you will learn that the person you relied upon yesterday isn't there today. Or they are there but are not answering when you call. Then they are present again. Then not. Your brain quickly realises that this person is not safe and so your anxiety will not be calmed by this person or any other. You find ways instead to self-soothe. You become happy in your own company. You rely only on yourself for nourishment: it's better not to expect, rather than be disappointed.

These traumas stick with you. They cannot be grown out of. The effects can be reduced, with the help of nurture and love, but this takes a very long time with enormous amounts of patience and strength from the adults involved.

This is a perfect explanation of why so many AdoptyChildren regularly struggle at school. Because there are so many people you are expected to trust, respect, obey, listen to, play nicely with, share with, tolerate, understand and simply rely upon, AdoptyBrains become frazzled. They find it too tricky to work out the genuine people and those who find tolerance too hard. Then when they start understanding that you truly can rely upon said person, they move up a year and start all over again.

This is to say nothing of everything else you have to cope with at school – staff leaving, other children, the many holidays, Father's day, Mother's day, Christmas, Easter, other religious activities, birthdays, school trips, inset days, supply teachers, academic grouping for lessons, play times, fallings-out with friends, rain, wind, sunshine, cake sales, puddles, play equipment, toys, boredom, reward charts, behaviour policies, chairs, PE kit, tellings-off, the fear of a telling-off, boyfriends, girlfriends, plays, nativities, assemblies, drama lessons, music lessons, shoes and school pets.

Every single one of these has caused one or both of my children to behave badly, push me away and cry hysterically at home. They may seem trivial, but to a traumatised brain, the smallest molehill can be a mountain. And the quicker the world understands this, the better these children will make their way through life.

Due to all the wobbly moments in school, we have found ourselves making happy moments by turning up to EVERYTHING! Class assemblies, open teaching sessions, fairs, coffee mornings, mother's and father's day meals, family games, movie nights – everything. This is tough as we both work long hours but when you see the children's faces as they notice you walk in, you know it's all worth it. At the previous school, AdoptyFamily even found ourselves winning the Halloween cake competition* two years in a row. First year we made a beautiful pumpkin chocolate bundt cake, drizzled with orange flavour icing topped with a green icecream cone, and the second time we made a full graveyard, with recently overturned soil (chocolate cake crumbled) and rich tea finger gravestones bearing the names of Elvis, Johnny Cash and one of the teachers. Oops! Must pay more attention! Both children were so proud of themselves, and fortunately these seem to be the memories they have kept from school, rather than dwelling on the negative ones.

* *Top tip for cake competitions: intentionally make cakes which are meant to be ugly. That way the kids can help, it looks like they have helped, and you win. Oh, and make them taste nice!*

Chapter 15

# Holidays

*Vacations don't
always help you unwind*

Holidays – I've no idea whether I love or hate them any more. In our lives as AdoptyParents we have been brave and ventured away from our home, for extended periods, several times. We've even managed trips abroad, much to our surprise!

Family holidays generally have a mix of happy and tricky moments with some parental relaxation and suntan smiles all round. When AdoptyFamily first travelled abroad we certainly did not achieve this – we had so many upsets that we forgot the point of a holiday and lived the rest of the days on edge. The flight home couldn't come soon enough.

As hinted at in previous chapters, Littlie has verbally abused a Spanish lady, attacked a Disneyland bus driver and gone missing in a theme park three times in one day.

Biggie has had major meltdowns, been drug searched at an airport and had a massive strop in the middle of a water park. I appreciate that these issues will ring true for many parents and you can all sigh and show me knowing smiles and kindly glances. However, our children are not behaving this way due to

**A**: Excitement

**B**: Lack of sleep

**C**: Sugar

They have a D option – which is that they are terrified

of going away. Biggie is recalling the past, when on several occasions his belongings were packed up for him – not for a holiday, but a move to yet another new home. At holiday time, he feels scared that we may be sending him away, even though we reassure that this is not the case. He is frightened that we may go away but then we might never come back. This hyper-vigilance has kept him safe in the past, so he will continue to act this way, even if it breaks every one of us.

Littlie is terrified that she will not know anyone on holiday. She won't know their names, so she can't communicate with them. Communication is her tool for safety. The more she talks, the cuter she becomes, the more friendly you are to her, the safer she is.

How can two parents possibly deal with the emotional stability and issues of two such wobbly bunnies? They are unwilling to talk and rationalise (even in their own way) and so put all their fear and anger into their behaviour – which is the last thing you need during a holiday.

I envy the dogs going to kennels – what a lovely quiet holiday they will have!

However – I plod on. After an explosion of one kind or another I sit, I ponder, I drink a cup of squash and I sigh, knowing that they don't mean to react that way, they do love me really and that I will love them eternally.

This was the way the first few school holidays went, so after a while we went for a change. We decided that structure was the key, so we tried a number of things.

**A holiday club** Disaster. We sooo over-prepared the venue for any difficulties that the staff were constantly calling out, 'Where is this one?' 'Keep an eye on him!' and even telling the parents waiting outside the gate, 'Sorry you're locked out, we have a potential runner!'

---

**Top tip for airports**

Special assistance is worth looking into when you fly. No one wants to share your child's meltdown, and it's your holiday too, so ask for the help. It really, really relieves the pressure at the start and end of your break away, and costs nothing.

---

**Bribery** – paying them to continue school work through the holidays. The rates – 20p to read a chapter in a book and a box of Lego for 20 pages written in textbooks. Littlie had to write 20 pages with at least one sentence on each – she was only four, so thought I wouldn't be too tough! This one went all right – both were accepting, although Biggie liked to give off a lot of moans.

I know this won't sit right with many parents who think kids shouldn't have to work in the holidays – and I do agree. However the pain of restarting school and the expectation to write is so huge that at least if we continue little bits here and there, it is not such a massive shock to the system.

**Stickers** A countdown to starting back at school. Both were keen to do this sticker-chart activity.

**Going out** – alternating home days with out-days. Even on a home day, scooting at the local park for a little bit. Made them feel like they've achieved something and made me a little less stir crazy as I may bump in to another human being to talk to!

This system didn't really work too well. Structure is only good if the children are happy to accept it, and while they like the familiarity of routine, many of the activities only appealed for a limited time. So we tried another strategy the following summer.

**Camping** There is no greater feeling of freedom than running through meadows and sand dunes, with the wind in your hair and a smile on your face – as the average clothing advert shows us. So that is what we decided to do.

We bought the tent, we borrowed equipment from seasoned camping professionals in the family and found a campsite to head to. We did our research – maximum journey time of 1.5 hours, freedom at every turn and free pitching

---

### Backseat winner

We have invented the most marvellous car game. If, like us, you suffer from constant car chatter due to anxiety, try this one.

"Let's play the quiet game. Whoever can be quiet the longest wins a marshmallow!" (Substitute your own organic treat if you prefer – I go with junk.) Our record is nine minutes before Biggie forgot, then eight minutes, then another six. It's so wonderful, I may patent it!

Another one – who can keep their eyes shut the longest? Best played with the under fours. Every time we played Littlie fell sound asleep for a nice daytime nap, awaking refreshed and much less angry. I did feel slightly guilty when she burst into tears and admitted that for the entire summer she had been cheating and actually had been asleep every time! Bless her. I shall save that one for when she is a mum herself!

---

rather than allocated spaces. It is nice to have neighbours but it's easy to get annoyed when AdoptyKids are screaming the site down and you are only 10 metres away.

Well, three days in we became a zero child family! We'd not done away with anyone or misplaced them, it's just we hardly saw them! Camping went well, even an indoor rainy day. The activity exhausted us all, so the kids were out for the count at 9pm – thank you, fresh air, for the gift you gave us! We had a couple of wobblies due to Littlie being exhausted. We soldiered on, ignoring any rude and silly behaviour (Adoptive Parenting 101 – pick your battles). And once we were treated to a three-hour nap in the back of the car that continued in the tent! She even asked to go to bed one night.

Biggie made some friends, in his usual in-their-face manner, but huge congrats to him for not being the loudest kid on the haystack! Biggie even told us he would rather one boy, who always wanted to talk to us during our meals, would stay away while we ate as it was embarrassing him. It may not seem it, but this was a huge breakthrough as Biggie is usually completely unaware of embarrassing behaviour and awkward social situations even while the rest of us are dying of shame.

This holiday far exceeded expectations. We were bonding, getting on mostly, with occasional mummy-bashing from Biggie –he wouldn't eat my delicious homemade jam because I'd made it – I pointed out this eliminated the majority of meals in his life.

We played games together, shared loving glances and touches. Biggie even coped with losing at every game, and not being allowed to spend his holiday money. If someone could have brought our dog over and sold our house, I don't think we would have come home. We finished most evenings with roasted marshmallows and a beer! This was so unexpected that we had to go and buy the equipment to enjoy this standard leisure activity, amazed that both children were calm enough to be allowed near a fire.

*

After this success, we decided to try a foreign holiday and a camping holiday this year. A week in Spain proved to us that the amount of progress which has been made is outstanding. There was no restraining anyone, no shouting abuse at strangers and no major meltdowns. True, Littlie threatened to smash her brother's face in, loudly and publicly of course, but I managed to calm her down. I asked her calmly what was upsetting her inside, and how we could solve that, or at least improve the feelings. As she is a girl after my own heart, we did this over cake, away from the 'smelly boys'. She loves the one-on-one time and it always helps soothe her hurting.

In fact, the holiday went so well that we would list our top complaint as noisy neighbours who came home drunk at 4am and partied till 5am. The next worst thing was the sticky heat, and then the arguments with the children – believe me, that's a HUGE improvement.

We didn't eat out, so no pressure there to behave, we lounged around watching as much TV as we wanted and spent many hours playing as a family in the pool. We all relaxed and got some much-needed bonding in, ready for the chaos of the rest of summer.

Camping this year is going to be short and sweet. We've planned a weekend at a free and easy campsite where our kids have been before. What is amazing is that we have been invited to camp with some friends and their child. People actually want to spend time with us and our kids! The mum is so understanding of Littlie and the way she works, and has encouraged a lovely friendship between her daughter and ours. I am hoping and praying for a filthy dirty, hay-playing, no-washing, beer-drinking, fire-building, marshmallow-toasting happy weekend! If you could cross your fingers too then I would really appreciate this ...

Chapter 16

# Returning to work

*I learn to juggle even more plates*

In my previous career I worked as a teacher. My hours were from 7.30am to 5.30pm. I would then drive home, and do marking and other work until 7pm. Then I cooked and ate dinner, and continued marking and planning until 10pm, by which time I would be falling asleep on my books. Weekends were spent researching, planning, marking, assessing and organising the next week.

And still I was told by one horrible headteacher that I didn't work hard enough. God bless the teachers still in the career, for they must not sleep!

It was obvious that adopting two demanding children and a teaching career wouldn't go easily. It might have been manageable, depending on the availability of my other half or support from the rest of the family, or if the children coped well with their new lives – but this was not to be for our family.

Just this week, when things haven't gone spectacularly wrong, I have attended two school meetings, one at 8am, one sports day, fielded three child-related phone calls, attended one paediatric appointment and sent seven emails regarding one or other child. And it's only Thursday morning.

If things are going badly at school, which is often the case, I can expect to receive more than 10 emails from one school, a couple of messages or phone calls from the other, more phone calls from the first school as well as having to make even more calls myself to arrange appointments. And don't forget the messages summoning me to pick up one child or the other because of their behaviour.

All of this, added to three hours a day commuting to and from their schools, which are each more than six miles away across an urban area, means I am one exhausted AdoptyMama.

You might think, why on earth does this loon send her children to schools so far away? And does she have to work?

Sadly, due the extensive emotional needs of both my kids, I had to choose schools which worked for them, not the closest. We started with the nearest one and as you will have read in Chapter 10, that one didn't go well!

Later we found a perfect primary school and happily drove 12 miles there and back every day, knowing that they were safe, happy and nurtured in an amazing supportive environment. The added complication came when Biggie moved up to secondary school, which added distance, cost, detentions, emails, meetings and phone calls to our lives! But we soldier on.

And yes I have to work. When my role was solely as AdoptyMum, I felt as though I was lost. I didn't have my own career any more, one which I had worked so hard for. I wasn't a fertile young woman, looking forward to the exciting times ahead. I wasn't a birth mum. I wasn't a mum friend at school, as practically no one spoke to me. I was AdoptyMum – but when things are going wrong, you don't feel like you are even doing that job well and I felt completely worthless.

So I looked for a new career without any idea as to what I could do. It needed to be flexible, fit around school times, be adaptable for school holidays, not too pressured time-wise, one I would be good at, and not too far away so I could get to school pick-up. Do such miracle job opportunities exist? Luckily, despite an initial rejection, I got a job in sales for a local media company. I work from home, I set my own hours – about two days a week – and I could manage the holidays really well. It was, and still is, perfect.

I am still in this job and it continues to give me the self confidence which is easily lacking as a parent and especially as an AdoptyParent.

My children frequently say they hate me and tell me I'm doing a terrible job. Sometimes they wish I'd never adopted them. The school problems make me feel as though I am failing as a parent. I hardly ever have time or energy to see friends, so that brings me down. It's really tough to wake up to ground level and begin a new day at zero when so many things bring you into negatives.

Happily my closest friends are AdoptyFriends or long-termers we've known for ages. AdoptyParents need no apologies, they aren't worried if the kids don't get along on that day, they look as exhausted and hairy as you do, and they bail on plans almost as frequently as they make them. But when I see them it is a laugh a minute at the ridiculous nature of our lives and we enjoy the precious time we have together.

Long termers – when I see them, it's like it's been minutes, not months, and so we don't waste time on the negatives, we jump straight into hysterical laughter, often accompanied by cocktails and dancing. Or sandpits and hot chocolate if the meet-up is in the local park! But it always feels as though we've never been apart and cheers my mood brilliantly.

So you can see I need to work. Just to give me a sense of myself again. I didn't like to feel lost. That was too hard and made me so unhappy. But since returning to work I feel more confident, happier, braver and able to handle more of what life throws at me. After all, how can this cup pour out love, support and consistency, if it is empty?

Chapter 17

# Predictability

*We learn the value of knowing what's going to happen*

As the years of parenting have gone on we have learnt more and more. Not just about different parenting styles, but about our children and their need for routine.

We are all aware of the events in a child's life where anxiety and excitement can occur – end of term, new school year, Christmas, birthdays, holidays and other 'fun' moments. At all these times kids can lose their heads and are susceptible to a range of emotions from extreme delight to devastation and tears.

However, with adopted children everything can cause this emotional upheaval. We've experienced either end of the extremes while playing the card game Uno, having new shoes, watching TV and trying new food. Once, at a regularly-visited restaurant, Biggie chose to stray from his standard menu choice into new territory. When his food came he couldn't stop giggling with anticipation and nerves. We captured a photo of the most beautiful smile on his face, knowing that he was excited, but so worried about him being disappointed. If I am honest, though, I too often choose the same food just so I know I won't be disappointed, so I can understand his concerns!

One thing we have learned is what gets under our kids' skins. We know more and more about what makes them tick, and what triggers strong emotions. Of course there are many times when we trigger these emotions and we ignore them, or misunderstand them. Or we parent in an unsympathetic, non-therapeutic way. We are only human and we are trying our best.

On the flip side, we are able to reflect on what we should have done and sometimes we remind each other of another strategy to try, without getting something aimed at our head by the other parent.

The old catchphrase 'touch wood' is essentially a curse in our home. If we say something and add 'touch wood', the thing we are dreading begins to happen.

Biggie was doing well at school – so AdoptyDad told our social worker, 'He seems to have settled in, touch wood.' Next day he threw a chair at someone!

'Littlie seems to have grown out of the night terrors at last, touch wood' … cue full-on horror movie screams as she woke up, and reacted like a cornered cat, hissing and scrambling to get away. She even threw a biscuit at my head rather than eat it!

We smile and discuss how well they've been getting on lately; cue the fisticuffs. No matter what the praise is, the fates find a way to encourage our children to sabotage it!

So we've realised we need to learn a parenting CPR system – Crazy Parenting Resources. Skills, tricks and items to swoop in with and save the situation or people involved. They look mad, they can be silly and embarrassing, they might be physical and often they bring filthy looks from bystanders who assume our children are getting away with murder. But on the day a kind and decent bystander offers a cheeky wink and a muttered 'great job', you'll feel as though you are floating on air and strutting to an imaginary beat. (My imaginary beat is Stayin' Alive' by the Bee Gees. More inspirational than Another One Bites the Dust!) AdoptyDad and I learn to predict when things are most likely to be difficult, and prepare ourselves. My handbag/backpack has become similar to that of the world's greatest childcare expert, Mary Poppins. Everything we might need is in there, lurking, waiting for its moment of glory.

We go to a restaurant and the food is delayed – out comes the pad of paper and pens, the miniature jigsaw or Rubik's cube. We go to a theme park and the queues are huge – out comes crunchy food and our Disability Living Allowance letters which allow us to jump to the front, preventing meltdown.

We cannot afford to be unprepared because we just fall flat on our faces – as you will see!

**Biggie and packed lunches** We assumed things were going fine. At no point had any of his caregivers or schools indicated there was a problem. Yet it turns out that the clever little monster was sneaking a handful of his lunch every time he left the classroom! He'd come in smelling of crisps with a satisfied smile on his face. His ingrained food survival skills were strong, needing to ensure he had a meal regardless of when he should be eating it.

Eventually we worked out that packed lunches just weren't the right thing; the staff disliked him eating whenever he wanted and so we've switched to school dinners.

If anyone knows how to stop him buying junk – please let me know. We are soon to be renaming him Biggie Cheesecake for the amount he's been consuming!

**Buses to school** We honestly believed Biggie could manage this. There's a dedicated school bus that goes directly to his school. He does have a 20-minute walk to get the bus but it calms him before school and his legs are as

> ## AdoptyMum's Patent Remedies for All Occasions
>
> **Nerves** - chewy sweets
> **Anger** - sucky sweets
> **Anxiety** - cuddly bunny toy
> **Fear** - sweet rewards if they can tell us their emotions
> **Selfishness** - extra toys to share
> **Lost items** - cuddles, and help looking.

long as grasshoppers! But due our being unprepared and to his unfortunate persistence at always being first, he began to get himself in mischief, competing with the older kids to get on first. After some pushing and shoving, threats and complaints, we decided that we needed a new plan.

Plan B was to catch public buses to school – miles cheaper for a start and there were more choices of which to take. Also they came with the added bonus of no children to compete with and lots of adults, who he is always polite to!

However, we did not prepare for the issues which we faced – full-up buses driving past without him, missed buses due to the terrible service, delayed buses due to traffic or the temptation of the local pub!

Yes, the pub, at age 11. I'll explain – he needed a wee, so he went in and asked to use the toilet. Sensible, I think! Then the kind-hearted landlord saw this sweaty boy and offered him a glass of water. No problem.

The next day Biggie needed the toilet

again! Hmmm, slightly dubious, but he does wee when he's bored and if the bus isn't coming then it seems logical.

Now you probably aren't too concerned at this point as he's not really doing anything too bad. However he then asked if he could have a drink ... they replied sure, water?

And that was their first mistake! You don't ask – you tell! Biggie politely replied, 'Hmmm, what am I allowed?' Biggie is notorious for pushing his luck, the grass is ALWAYS greener and he sulks about what he might be missing.

This is how my son began drinking regular pints of lemonade in the pub, free of charge! As you can imagine, when we found out we were horrified at the risks he was facing, not to mention the ridiculous behaviour of the pub who hadn't even informed the school that one of their pupils was practising the art of blagging.

I went to the pub to point out that they really should tell someone about visits from random children ... and to explain that if they ever see my son again, they are to kick him up the arse and tell him 'I'm calling your mother!'

When I got there, several old boys were at the bar drinking a pint of their usual from their own glasses. Overhearing me tell the owner not to serve my son any more, one of the regulars piped up: 'Awww, you ain't stopping our boy coming in are you? We like that young 'un!'

I left shaking my head, wondering what planet I was living on. Surely this was worthy of a TV comedy sketch?

Biggie, of course, couldn't understand why we were so worried. I'm sure I aged about a decade in that conversation.

Another thing we were not prepared for was Littlie's unpredictable sense of humour. As I've said, she is a young Peter Kay with comedic timing, wit and quick thinking. She's got great dance moves which she uses to her advantage.

Often when you're annoyed at her, and trying to tell her something, she throws you a shimmy of the shoulders and you have to try your best not to laugh.

The first time she swore, aged three, she shouted to her brother 'Why are you being so shitty today?' To be honest, she had a good point.

## Chapter 18

# Dad view

*AdoptyDad speaks*

When asked to put pen to paper for this book two things came to mind. The first is how much I have learned during our journey with our children. The second is how difficult it is to watch the person that you love suffer at the hands of someone else that you love: a small person who doesn't understand why they find life so difficult.

I love nothing more than to learn something new. As an academic, I have made a career out of learning and helping others to learn. When AdoptyMum and I started this adoption journey I never imagined that there was so much to learn that I didn't even know existed. I thought that children who had suffered neglect, loss or trauma early in life simply required a couple of years of love, and all would be well. I thought I was about to engage in a worthwhile journey that would be fun for all.

In my day job at a university, I am sometimes asked to produce publicity material that sums up the experience of learning. The first image that comes to mind for me (and I suspect for many of us) is of a child with a smile of wonder on their face, as they experience something new to them. Perhaps they are looking at a test tube close up or are overjoyed at some fire erupting from nowhere. My experience of real learning on the adoption journey feels very different.

It is one thing to read a textbook, or sit in a classroom and listen to someone talk about their area of expertise, but this is not how I believe the important lessons are learned. The best learning experiences are often when we are feeling vulnerable or utterly lost. Rarely when I am learning something do I sit with a big smile on my face wondering joyfully at the mystery that is unravelling in front of me. It is more likely that I will have reached the limit of my ability to work something out, while being in a situation where not working it out is NOT an option. This kind of learning involves real risk, whether that be to our bodies, our minds, our hearts, our view of ourselves or our ability to keep on with whatever we are doing.

The point I am trying to make is that this learning is not something that you get given by a book or an expert. It is something that comes from living it in the moment. It often feels as if my children are the teachers in the classroom of adoptive parenting, and I am the pupil sat bewildered and unsure what to do. The smile and the wonder comes much later – sometimes days, sometimes weeks – and in some cases I am still waiting for that moment to come.

In the last five years I have been put in this situation on a weekly and sometimes daily basis. While it leaves you scarred, those scars feel as if they are worthwhile, like they not only left you better informed about the world, but that they were the whole point of it. This is why I am so excited to see the story of the last five years of our lives recorded in this book as a series of journeys. Each journey brought its own sadness, playfulness, inquisitiveness and sense of reflection.

If I can give one piece of advice to anyone adopting or fostering children, or engaging in anything similarly unpredictable and emotionally taxing, it is 'Write it down!' For me writing things down, not eloquently or even with the intention that it be read later on, is a life saver. When you are helping a child deal with a complex trauma, it is so easy to feel overwhelmed that you are not getting anywhere. But writing out your experience helps you to focus your thoughts in the moment, and keep things in perspective.

Writing this book, and an earlier blog, has been AdoptyMum's way of releasing the pressure put on her by our family's journey. She sits at the computer and writes from her heart. No agonising over what words to use, no re-visiting the stories that she told, she just writes and moves on. I have watched her draw immense pleasure from being able to convey the difficulties of our lives. This has helped her develop a confidence in dealing with the complex aspects of our children's lives that I haven't seen come so easily in any other way. And for me, reading her stories and interpretations has given me a completely different perspective on the experiences that I have had. This was really important for me, as watching AdoptyMum having to deal with the daily traumas has been tough.

My wife has covered so many pieces of the adoptive parenting puzzle that I struggled to think what I could give that she hadn't already described far more eloquently. There is something, however, that she cannot reflect upon as I can, and that is the struggle of watching her experience this journey and the traumas it brings every day. You need to understand that she and I sit at the opposite ends of the emotional, organisational and practical spectrum in almost every way. This was so apparent that it formed a reasonable portion of the questions asked us by the adoption panel. AdoptyMum is pragmatic, outgoing, trusting, in-the-moment, carefree and wears her heart on her sleeve. I, however, think far too long about everything before doing it (if I actually do anything). I am introverted, pretty controlling, I worry about everything and am fiercely independent. Don't worry, I'm not as bad as all that! I do have a remarkable ability to see the same situation from a range of perspectives. Anyway, we saw our differences as our strength, not our weakness, and told our adoption panel as much. And by and large this has turned out to be true.

Being so different, however, means that the things that often go unnoticed by one of us stand out like a sore thumb to the other. For my wife, adoption has certainly brought out the best in her. I see her absolute love of life and mischievous nature reflected in the gappy smile and giggles of my daughter. I see that after day upon day of rejection she continues to try to build a relationship with a son who struggles to understand that she is not trying to replace the parent that he knew and lost early in his life. Experiencing and recovering from this repeatedly is tough. It is not the same as putting the door back on its hinges or picking up the broken toys, plates and torn up memories. It sticks ... and it drains you. What makes it so difficult is that it feels deliberate, directed, manipulative and unending. The reality that I see is that the hurt is almost entirely unintentional, and understandable, but that it can drain the life and soul out of you without you noticing it.

Watching this story play out day after day, often without any recognisable benefit, is painful. AdoptyMum won't be able to see this happening; her nature is not to dwell on it but to bounce back the next day and try something new. But it does take its toll. I watch her feeling it, in the evenings when the kids are in bed and she is exhausted. For the last couple of years this is the area of adoption that I have yet do any real learning about. My desire to try to fix the problem for her or to offer the "correct" point of view, rather than support her through her struggle, means that I often miss the most useful thing about being her partner, to offer empathy and comfort. Ironically, my experience has been that the healing from the secondary trauma that she has experienced has come not from us sitting down and analysing every problem in infinite detail. Instead it has been to allow her to stop dwelling on it, forget it in some cases and do something together that reminds you why you began the journey in the first place. As an engineer, it is almost impossible not to break down the problems that I have in front of me and tackle each one in an orderly manner. But parenting children with complex traumas is not predictable and analysable. It requires you to have an accepting and open mind that can respond in the moment, not according to a recipe.

There is no shortcut to helping children with complex traumas to understand and heal themselves, so you might as well get your hands dirty and enjoy as much of it as you can. Your children will benefit far more from it and learn far more from you if you do. Thanks, AdoptyMum, for allowing me to realise this before it was too late.

Chapter 19

# Five years on

*We look back – and forward*

We are now five years into the chaotic frenzy of being an AdoptyFamily. Littlie is well in to junior school, loving music and dancing, Little Mix and Bieber (groan), while Biggie is causing mayhem at a secondary school which was just not ready for him and so finds it tough to manage his anxieties.

AdoptyDad is battling health and work as always, but is generally succeeding, and me – well it's a case of same old same old really, working while preparing myself for the summer holidays and the return to school that's quickly approaching. But with the added hoorah moments that I now part-own the company I work for, and I've written a book! Oh, and the AdoptyPets are happy enough with lots of love and affection from both children on an almost hourly basis.

Writing this book has given me many opportunities to reflect over the past. And it's struck me that I haven't thought to the far future very often.

Biggie wants to do every job under the sun – he genuinely believes he can drive a train at night while attending school in the day after buying his own huge house. He doesn't see the point in doing homework, as it won't help him in the future when he is an engineer and running a bread factory. It's crazy how his dreams intertwine. Littlie wants to be a pop star, with archeologist as a back-up.

I think the reason we AdoptyParents don't think about our

### Friends – The Sequel

Friendships are something my kids still find difficult. Littlie can make friends easily, she's charming, fun to play with and not too bossy. But can she keep them?

Biggie on the other hand can't make friends. He plays immaturely and is very controlling. He will play any game – as long as it's his way and he's in charge!

Usually kids grow out of bossiness or silly play. However, adopted children have such a need to control that the give-and-take of friendship is difficult for them. With girls, being bossy tends to cause fights, but boys just drift away as they don't want to be told what to do. Immaturity in games can work well with kindred spirits but at school, teachers quickly intervene and the frequent scoldings cause parents to advise their offspring to stay away from the child who keeps getting them in trouble.

With Littlie we have regular tears about how she's fallen out with this one or that one. She just can't understand why the child is unhappy with her. Yet she doesn't notice her own role in the name calling or taking sides. She's a people pleaser and it doesn't occur to her that when she's standing up for one friend, she's being mean to another.

dreams is because we have to live very much in the present. Too much forward planning leads to disappointment, upset and expensive mistakes. There's only so many times we can book a babysitter and have to cancel her due to family chaos, losing our allotted hours for yet another month. In a perfect

Biggie now has many children who like him. Most people he invites do come to his birthday parties. In fact this year's was a roaring success with calmness, enjoyment and zero tantrums.

But sadly, even though he's a nice kid to know and makes people laugh, he doesn't seem to have close friends. He's instantly forgotten by others when they choose a partner to spend time with or to invite round. He's always waiting for the moment someone remembers him.

Obviously I help and invite people to play, and tag along to events with both kids, but it's not the same.

The day he received his first invitation to a birthday party – the first where I'd played no role in orchestrating the invitation – was sheer happiness. His little face beamed for many hours after he proudly raced to show us the treasured piece of paper.

Littlie used to be invited to lots of parties and always had a lovely time but these days the invitations seem only to come from the boys in her class, as she can't seem to stop arguing with the girls. Fingers crossed this is something that will calm down as she grows up, but I don't hold out much hope if I'm honest. She could start an argument in an empty room ...

world I would like to believe that we can look forward to the kids moving out, and to weddings and babies in the distance. In fact, I have shared many a conversation with Littlie about this. Believe it or not, she has created her own birthing plan in which the doctor gives her sleepy medicine (anaesthetic) and then just takes the baby from her while daddy holds her hand. Her partner can't be in the room because they shouldn't see her naked, as that's rude!

But due to their anxieties, difficulties, quirks and downright weirdness at times, life is bound to be an uphill battle for them. How can they find others willing to adapt to their way of thinking and reacting, and more importantly, keep those people in their lives?

But if I look at how far they have come so far, I begin to feel reassured. When they became engrained in our lives, they were both feisty, wild little people with refusals and tantrums at every turn. They didn't love us and hardly knew what love was. Yet with masses of perseverance those two little bunnies began to feel what love meant, through support, regular meals, comfort, excitement, happiness, and verbal and physical reminders.

They have achieved so much so far in many areas of their lives. Tantrums are far less common, and if there is a meltdown, we can generally manage it in under an hour rather than four or five hours. The two of them can play together and get along, rather than just fighting and biting. They care about one another, worrying when Littlie is sick or Biggie is away overnight, and they show their love in their own individual ways.

No longer do we restrain the children for their own safety on a regular basis. They can both talk about how they are feeling, and both can explain how the other has made them feel. They are making academic progress slowly but surely. Teachers are beginning to enjoy teaching Biggie, and they feel like they understand our family. The foster family are never mentioned by school staff, and the birth family only in context, when asking about their previous lives.

Biggie is far more reserved than his sister. He has been left brokenhearted so often that he guards his love and prefers to offer charm and affection rather than deeper emotions. But we know it is in there deep down.

Littlie gushes with love. It is awkward sometimes just how often she compliments me in one day. At one class assembly she had several parents in tears (as well as me) during a rendition of the Beatles' *All You Need Is Love* as she shouted across the room, 'You mama, I mean you, I love you!' She tells all of us how much she loves us all the time. Her dreams are filled with adventures with us, and her nightmares are always ones where Mama has left her and gone away without her.

So if you use the amount of love given and received as a measure of how successful this adoption life has been so far – then we are doing a bloody brilliant job. And I guarantee – so are you!

# Useful resources

I wrote this book because I didn't find anything else which reflected my experience as an in-at-the-deep-end parent of two lovely but troubled AdoptyKids. But there are plenty of books and other resources which AdoptyDad and I have found to be helpful, useful or real lifesavers.

## For parents

*The A-Z Therapeutic Parenting: Strategies and Solutions*
**Sarah Naish** Jessica Kingsley Publishers ISBN 10 1785923765

Sarah Naish is a social worker and experienced foster parent, but when she adopted five children she found that all her experience had not equipped her to cope with the traumas the children had arrived with. Now she has drawn up an A-Z guide to 60 common problems parents face, from acting aggressively to difficulties with sleep, with advice on what might trigger these issues, and how to respond.

This is the adoptive parents' bible. Simply the greatest tool for emergency help. Look up your topic by title and there is some great advice for a whole range of issues.

*First Steps in Parenting the Child Who Hurts*
*Next Steps in Parenting the Child Who Hurts*
**Caroline Archer** Jessica Kingsley Publishers
ISBN 1-85302-801-0, ISBN 1-85302-802-9

Great introductions for the issues we have faced as our children grow and change. Makes suggestions about what you can expect at each age group, and helped us realise that certain issues we were struggling with were normal.

*Happiest Toddler on the Block*
**Harvey Karp** Bantam Books ISBN 0-553-38143-1
This gave us great hints and ideas of how to bond with our new toddler and emotionally immature older child.

*The Unofficial Guide to Adoptive Parenting*
**Sally Donovan** Jessica Kingsley Publishers ISBN 13 978-1849055369
Lots of great life examples to spot the textbook ideas in context. Helpful to know what might be coming!

*No Matter What*
**Sally Donovan** Jessica Kingsley Publishers ISBN 13 978-1849054317
Stories about a family building their lives together from a young age. Frames what adopting is like rather than advice.

*Building the Bonds of Attachment: Awakening Love in Deeply Troubled Children*
**Dan Hughes** Rowman & Littlefield ISBN-10: 1442274131
Dan Hughes is an expert on attachment theory and and this is a great real-life case study of an adopted child. It's easy to follow, and useful to see behaviour and trauma in the context of attachment. Points out that the other parent needs reminding that they are doing a great job.

*A Day with Dan Hughes*
**Dan Hughes** Video recording, Falkirk 2009
vimeo.com/292109115
Here Dan talks through the many types of attachment and why conventional parenting and therapy won't work. Also a great section on how to speak to a child.

## For kids

*Blame my Brain*
**Nicola Morgan** Walker Books ISBN 978-1-4063-4693-0

A great way to get a teen to understand their brain. Helping them understand why parents do what they do – especially if you feel like you're talking to a brick wall.

*My Hidden Chimp*
**Professor Steve Peters** Studio Press Books
ISBN 978 1-78741-371-9

A guide to help a child understand why they react in certain ways when others might not. A book to read with your child of 10 upwards to help them manage their emotions and behaviour.

Smart Girl's Guides
*A Smart Girl's Guide ... To Friendship Troubles*
Published by American Girl ISBN 978-1-60958-223-4
*A Smart Girl's Guide ... To Liking Herself*
ISBN 978-1-59369-943-7
*A Smart Girl's Guide ... To Drama, Rumours and Secrets*
ISBN 978-1-60958-903-5
*A Smart Girl's Guide ... To Knowing What To Say*
ISBN 978-1-59369-772-3

All four books are really helpful to talk through with girls aged 8-11. Makes them realise that everyone goes through these things, and they are not alone.

## Films and TV

*Adoption at the Movies*
**adoptionlcsw.com**

A regularly-updated blog which alerts you to children's films with themes or incidents which might upset AdoptyKids (see Chapter 8).

*The Loud House* Nickelodeon
nick.co.uk/shows/loud-house

A great short TV show about a family with one boy and 10 girls. Useful examples of ways to deal with life's difficulties in practical, moral and child-friendly ways – always as a family.

*Inside Out* Pixar
pixar.com/feature-films/inside-out

A brilliant animated movie about the variety of feelings inside a child's head and how they all need to work in tandem, otherwise chaos, upset and anger occurs. Really helpful to explain to a younger child about how their brain has different emotions in it.

# Room for thoughts, feelings and funny bits

# Room for thoughts, feelings and funny bits

# Room for thoughts, feelings and funny bits

ADOPTYMUM